THE LITTLE BOOK OF LIVERPOOL

THE
LITTLE
BOOK
OF
LIVERPOOL

ALEXANDER TULLOCH

The
History
Press

First published 2011
Reprinted 2012, 2014, 2019, 2021

The History Press
97 St George's Place,
Cheltenham, GL50 3QB
www.thehistorypress.co.uk

British Library Cataloguing in Publication Data.
A catalogue record for this book is available from the British Library.

ISBN 978 0 7524 6006 2

Typesetting and origination by The History Press
Printed by Imak, Turkey

CONTENTS

INTRODUCTION

If you were born on Mars you might not have heard of Liverpool. And if you were born on Mars you might have difficulty naming a famous Liverpudlian or two. Otherwise you've got no excuse; you should be able to reel off singers, footballers, actors, writers, entrepreneurs or politicians who hail from 'the Pool' almost without thinking about it. After all, every time you open a newspaper or turn on the telly you don't have to wait long before you see or hear something or someone to remind you of one of the most renowned cities, not just in Britain, but in the whole world.

Name any field of human endeavour and you will nearly always find the Liverpudlians have been there. Without Liverpudlians the world of literature, sport, television, the railways, the theatre, politics, medicine etc., etc. would have been at least very different and in all probability much the poorer. The vast mixing bowl of Liverpool has had ingredients poured into it from all over the world and the result is a rich mixture of nationalities, languages, skin colours, customs, ideas, talents and regional accents that have all blended to produce something unique. And that unique concoction is the witty, down-to-earth Scouser.

But there was another influence: adversity. These days the resurrection of the city is much vaunted in the newspapers and on television, but even within living memory it was a very different story. The conditions in which many people lived in Liverpool not so long ago were, by today's standards, appalling. The overcrowding, the squalor, the hunger and the violence took a heavy toll among the rapidly expanding population, particularly in the nineteenth century, but those who survived proved that poverty can be both a harsh master and a good teacher. Liverpudlians themselves used to say that if you could survive in Liverpool you could survive anywhere. There might be a slight exaggeration here but not too much and there are many of Liverpool's sons (and daughters) who have come from very humble beginnings and gone on to achieve great things. The contribution Scousers have made to British and world culture is undeniable.

When the author of this book was a boy, Liverpool was associated just about everywhere else in Britain with poverty, crime, bomb sites and slums – and, to be honest, the city still has many problems. But to most people born after the 1950s the city is synonymous with The Beatles, comedians, music, first-class football and gripping television drama. And of course, it is now also a byword for some of the most exciting new architecture in the world. Liverpudlians can now speak with pride of Liverpool One, undeniably among the finest examples in the land of what can be achieved in the field of renovation, reconstruction and architectural renaissance. The grimy Paradise Street of a generation ago has been swept aside. Now visitors and residents alike can shop, have a meal or just sit at a continental-style pavement café and enjoy a coffee and croissant (or possibly even a 'wet Nellie' – see p.11) in clean and pleasant surroundings. Or, if they prefer, they can move a few yards away from the bustling urban activity and sit in a thoughtfully designed park, switch off and indulge in the delightful pastime of just watching the world go by.

But that is not all. The planners have also transformed the Pier Head. When the plans for the new waterfront were first published many people had their misgivings. The already iconic Three Graces were to be joined by futuristic, experimental architecture which, it was feared, would be totally out of keeping with its surroundings. But the fears have been proven groundless. The old and the new blend together harmoniously and King Edward VII, astride his trusty steed, appears quite unruffled by the changes that have been taking place all around him over the last decade or so. The only slight misfit now is Our Lady & St Nicholas's Church, built on the site of St Mary del Key, the thirteenth-century church by the water's edge. This stately reminder of the very earliest days of the little hamlet that developed over 800 years into a mighty port now looks a little forlorn and overawed by her surroundings. Once she dominated the skyline and was a beacon to homeward bound sailors; now it is her turn to be put in the shade by surrounding hotels and high-rise commercial buildings. Like a graceful dowager duchess almost obscured by her taller sons and grandsons, she must accept her more lowly status, but then this is progress. Liverpool has changed enormously, as has the world. And the world, in many respects, has been changed by Scousers.

Now, something of an apology. When I accepted the challenge of putting this book together, I knew there would be no shortage of material on which to draw as the city where I was born is a veritable gold-mine of historical, social and cultural information. But I confess that I did not realise just *how* rich that goldmine would turn out to be. Consequently there are no doubt many people, places, events and facts which I have left out, either intentionally or unintentionally, which readers feel I ought to have included. If such omissions are seen as a defect, I can only say in my own defence that there is a limit to what you can cram into 50,000 words.

LIVERPOOL HUMOUR: EXAMPLE ONE

'He'll pay yer back that fiver when Nelson gets 'is eye back'
You'll never see that £5 you lent him again

1

JUST FOR STARTERS
. . . SOME TRIVIA

'Liverpool' is just the most recent spelling in a long list of variants. In the eleventh century it was either *Lytherpool* or *Lyrpool*. In the twelfth, *Litherpool* appeared and then, by the reign of King John (1167–1216) we find *Lyrpul*. Then there was a whole succession of different spellings: *Liverpolle, Liverpull, Lierpull* and, by the sixteenth/seventeenth centuries, *Lyrpole, Lyverpoole* and *Leverpool*.

The American poet Allen Ginsburg (1926–97) referred to Liverpool as being 'the centre of consciousness of the human universe.'

Liverpool is the only city on mainland UK to have elected an Irish Nationalist MP. In 1885 Thomas Power O'Connor was elected to represent the then Liverpool constituency of Liverpool Scotland (the Scotland Road area) at Westminster.

Liverpudlians used to be referred to as 'Liverpolitans'.

The land on which the Adelphi Hotel now stands used to be a pleasure garden where the better-off residents strolled and listened to music on fine summer evenings.

'Adelphi' is Greek for 'brothers'. The name was chosen because the hotel was built on the site of a former country home owned by two brothers and it was intended to preserve their association with the hotel by referring to them in its name.

In the seventeenth century there were so many salmon fished around Garston that they were fed locally to the pigs.

The clock on the Liver Building was timed to start at the precise moment the crown was placed on King George V's head at his coronation on 22 June 1911. The clock's nick-name is 'Great George', presumably by analogy with London's 'Big Ben'.

The very first Woolworth's store in Britain was opened at 25–25a Church Street, Liverpool, on 5 November 1909.

Liverpool, like many coastal towns, has a church dedicated to St Nicholas and there is a particular reason for this. St Nicholas was the patron saint of children, which is why he is remembered as Father Christmas. However, he was also the patron saint of thieves, sailors and smugglers and so was popular among sea-faring folk. It also explains why stealing or being caught stealing is referred to in English slang as 'nicking' or being 'nicked'.

Liverpool has its own 'Holy Land', a part of Toxteth so called because the street names are decidedly biblical – Moses Street, Isaac Street, Jacob Street and David Street. There is also a little stream called the Jordan and a farm called Jericho Farm.

Paradise Street takes its name from an Old Persian word *pairidaeza* meaning nothing more than 'walled garden or park'.

Chavasse Park, the breathing space for Liverpudlians at the centre of Liverpool One, is named after a prominent local family. Francis James Chavasse was Bishop of Liverpool from 1900 to 1923.

Scotland Road, which now looks more like an urban motorway, used to be a thriving tight-knit community with shops of every kind and a pub on every corner.

Exchange station on Tithebarn Street closed in 1977 but the splendid façade is still there today. The First World War poet and author Siegfried Sassoon often stayed in the adjacent hotel and it was here that he wrote *A Soldier's Declaration* in July 1917. This was a forthright attack on those politicians and generals who had the power to end the war but chose not to.

WHAT'S A WET NELLIE?

Officially a Nelson Cake, a gooey, sweet Scouse delicacy made from stale cake or bread.

THE LIVER BIRDS

The Liver Birds on top of the Liver Building are 18ft tall, have a wing span of 24ft and are made of copper. They were designed by a German sculptor, one Carl Bernard Bartels, who was living in England before the First World War. As a way of saying 'thank you', when the war started the police arrested Bartels and he was interned on the Isle of Man as an enemy alien. Although he had a wife in London, when the war was over the poor man was sent back to Germany and all reference to his achievement was erased from the record books. Is that gratitude or what?

THE TRAM

If you want to have a look at Liverpool's very last tram you still can. Unfortunately, however, you will have to travel all the way to America as that's where it is now on display. It was built in

A once ubiquitous Liverpool tram.

1939 and known as the Baby Grand, presumably because of its rather bulbous appearance. After it had trundled for the last time through the city's streets, in September 1957, it was shipped out to the USA where it was handed over to the Seashore Trolley Museum in Kennebunkport, Maine, in 1958. It is still there today along with similar exhibits from places as far afield as Leeds, Berlin, Glasgow and Nagasaki.

LIVERPOOL HUMOUR: EXAMPLE TWO

'She's all fur coat an' no drawers'
She likes to behave like royalty but in fact she's as poor as everyone else

NOT SO VERY LONG AGO IN LIVERPOOL

Lifts in the posh stores were manned by 'lift attendants'.

Boys wore short trousers until they were about thirteen.

Hospitals had strict visiting hours.

Cinemas had matinee performances for children on Saturdays. They were usually known as the 'kids' crushes'.

Buses all had a driver and a conductor who issued tickets to travellers. It was also his job to ring the bell to tell the driver when to stop and start. Female conductors were known as 'clippies'.

Buses were either 'Corpy' (Corporation), Ribble or Crosville. The Corpy buses were green, the Ribble ones red and the Crosville buses green and yellow.

Houses all had open fires and the coal was delivered by horse-drawn carts.

Kids who passed the 11+ and went to grammar school all had to study Latin or Greek or both.

Every November the city was shrouded in dense smog and all traffic came to a stand-still.

Neighbours would come round with monotonous regularity to borrow a cup of sugar.

All schoolgirls wore gymslips.

Grammar school teachers always wore academic gowns.

Shops closed all day on Sundays and on Wednesday afternoons.

£1 would buy you 4 gallons of petrol.

The *Liverpool Echo* was a broadsheet.

People on limited incomes would go to green grocers' shops and ask for 'fades', i.e. fruit and veg past their best and being sold cheap.

The post was always delivered twice a day and there was even a delivery on Christmas Day.

The only radio stations were the BBC's Home Service, the Light Programme and Radio Three. For popular music there was only Radio Luxembourg. Radio Merseyside and Radio City were not even a dream when The Beatles burst onto the scene.

You could sail from Liverpool to New Brighton on the *Royal Iris* or the *Royal Daffodil*.

You could buy flowers from Lizzie Christian who had a stall on Clayton Square for over sixty years.

Kids in school were caned for bad behaviour, being late or just for handing in unsatisfactory work.

Boy scouts, Cubs and the Boys' Brigade were expected to attend Church Parade one Sunday per month and march along the roads behind standard-bearers, buglers and drummers.

Rag and bone men were a frequent sight.

Most churches organised 'socials' on Saturday nights.

Milk floats and bread vans were horse-drawn.

Housewives cleaned the front steps with 'donkey stones'.

Many of the streets were still cobbled.

Horses' drinking troughs were still a common sight.

As late as the 1960s street lighting still relied largely on the old gas lamps which had to be lit individually every evening. On 20 August 1819 the following notice appeared in the *Liverpool Mercury*:

'The Liverpool Gas Light Company is desirous of contracting with a respectable person, at a price per Lamp, for one year commencing 11th September next, to light and Extinguish all such Public Gas Lamps as shall be put up in the course of a year: and to keep them well cleaned and in repair. For full particulars applications are to be made to the Company's Office Dale Street, where sealed tenders will be received on or before Friday August 27th at seven o'clock in the evening.

By Order of the Committee
Charles ROWLINSON Secretary

Knife-grinders called regularly to sharpen kitchen knives and scissors on a revolving stone wheel in the back of a van. Kids would stand and watch, mesmerised by the showers of sparks flying off the wheel.

The 'nit nurse' visited schools on a regular basis to examine children's hair for head lice.

Kids who were off school for more than a day or two were visited by a man from the School Board. His job was to make sure any absence from school was for a genuine reason.

WHAT DO YOU CALL SOMEONE FROM LIVERPOOL?

The oldest term, and one that has fallen from use now, is 'Dickey Sam'. It is just possible that this is because Liverpudlians were associated with a ship of the same name in the eighteenth century, but we cannot be sure. We are not even sure which came first, the ship or the epithet. Another explanation is that the term derives from a certain Richard Samuels who was the landlord of an inn on Mann Island in the eighteenth century.

Another term is 'wack' or 'wacker'. Again we cannot say for sure but it could well date back to the influx of Gaelic-speaking Irish in the nineteenth century or even earlier. The Irish for 'my son' is 'mo mhac' pronounced 'mo wack'.

The most common term now, of course, is 'Scouse' or 'Scouser'. We do know that this is because of the presumed association by outsiders of Liverpudlians with their traditional dish: scouse or lobscouse. This hearty fare was imported by the Dutch and Scandinavian sailors who used to visit the port in days gone by. These nations all have a variant of 'lapskovs', a mushy cheap stew which was avidly adopted by the people of Liverpool. And the first syllable, 'lob' is cognate with the German 'labbig' meaning 'sloppy'.

SPRING-HEELED JACK

In the first half of the nineteenth century people all over the country began to report being attacked by a strange creature who had all the appearances of a human together with certain animal attributes and a few supernatural ones as well. He had red eyes, could breathe out blue or white smoke and had sharp steel-like fingers. But the most alarming characteristic was the creature's ability to jump great heights. He also had a nasty habit of attacking lone young women, smothering them with kisses at the same time as ripping their clothes with his long, sharp fingernails.

The first sightings of this 'gentleman' were in London, but soon he was reported in places such as Sheffield and the Midlands. Then, in 1888 he was supposedly 'sighted' in Everton, on the roof of St Francis Xavier's Church in Salisbury Street. He was last reported in 1904 when he is supposed to have made an appearance in William Henry Street.

PADDYWAGON

A common name for a police van (Black Maria) in Liverpool was a 'paddywagon' and there are two explanations for the origin of the term. The first is that the term was an import from New York where so many of the police were immigrant Irish that the official cars they drove were named after the drivers' place of origin. The other is that in Liverpool the vans were christened 'paddywagons' because the police frequently used them for conveying drunken Irishmen back to the cells.

LIVERPOOL HUMOUR: EXAMPLE THREE

'If 'ee wuz a ghost 'ee wouldn't give yer a fright'
He is very careful with his money

DID YOU KNOW?

Calderstones Park in Allerton is an ancient burial ground that is thought to pre-date even Stonehenge in Wiltshire. The 'calder stones', from which the park takes its name, are thought to have religious significance and date from about 3000 BC.

Former pupils of Liverpool College (a co-educational public school and member of the Head Masters' Conference) are known as 'Old Lerpoolians'.

In August 2001 Liverpool as a city made a public and contrite apology for the role it had played in the slave trade.

The children's construction kit which we now know as Meccano was originally named Mechanics Made Easy. A patent for the design was taken out by Liverpudlian Frank Hornby in 1901. He was born in Copperas Hill in 1863.

The only assassinated British Prime Minister, Spencer Perceval (1762–1812), was shot dead in the House of Commons in May 1812 by John Bellingham (1769–1812), a merchant who had his office in Duke Street, Liverpool.

From 1780 to 1796 the MP for Liverpool was a certain Bamber Gascoigne of Childwall, a direct descendant of whom is Bamber Gascoigne, the television personality and original host of TV's *University Challenge.*

Liverpool One, the shining new 'jewel in the crown' of Liverpool, occupies land used to fill in much of the original 'pool' that gave the city its name. The cost of building this gleaming shopping centre in the early years of the twenty-first century was £920,000,000 – give or take a few pounds.

Because of its unusual shape the Catholic cathedral in Liverpool is referred to locally as 'Paddy's Wigwam' or 'the Mersey Funnel'.

Gerard Houllier, the former manager of Liverpool Football Club, began his life in England as a teacher at Alsop High School, Queens Drive, from 1969 to 1970.

William Gladstone (1809–98), four times Prime Minister of Great Britain, was born at 62 Rodney Street. The street is now largely occupied by medical specialists and is widely thought of as the Harley Street of the north.

In Liverpool a 'seg' is what people everywhere else refer to as a 'callus' (i.e hardened skin) usually found on the hands. It is also a term used sarcastically by Scousers to describe people who are work-shy and only show up after the hard work has been done.

The Liverpool Bumblebee Haven Project was set up in 2010 to help stop the decline in their numbers. The aim is to create new bee-friendly habitats in an urban environment.

The man who first introduced the British public to the delights of the humble banana is thought to be Sir Alfred Jones (1845–1909), a Liverpool ship owner.

Brownlow Hill used to be called Poorhouse Lane.

The actress, model and 'Bond Girl' Halle Berry is half American, half British. Her mother was born in Liverpool.

Liverpool has one of the oldest Chinatowns in the country. Chinese sailors began settling in the city in the 1860s and established a community which still thrives in the city today.

Liverpool Chinese
Christian
Disciples Church
基督門徒教會
星 期 日 上 午   **11.00 am Sunday Service**

An example of the many signs written in English and Chinese in Liverpool's Chinatown.

The West Tower, which cost £35,000,000 to build, is one of the latest additions to Liverpool's waterfront. It boasts 40 floors and is 459ft high. Previously the tallest building in the city was St John's Beacon at 452ft while the Royal Liver Building, by comparison, is a mere stripling at 300ft.

The motto on Liverpool's coat of arms – *deus nobis haec otia fecit* – is usually translated as 'God has bestowed these blessings on us'.

The motto of the University of Liverpool is *haec otia studia fovent* ('such leisure encourages study') and that of Liverpool John Moores University is *audentes fortuna juvat* ('Fortune assists the bold').

The connection between mosquitoes and malaria was discovered by Sir Ronald Ross (1857–1932), Professor of Tropical Medicine at the Liverpool School of Tropical Medicine. His research into the disease was conducted there and in India between the 1890s and 1902.

An early advertisement for a once well-known store in Liverpool shows that the 'grocer's apostrophe' has not always been with us. The Bon Marché claimed in the early 1900s that they sold 'Everything for Ladies' and Gentlemen's, Girls' and Boys' Wear'. No sign of a misplaced apostrophe anywhere!

Sir Terence Rattigan, author of *The Winslow Boy* and *The Browning Version*, taught Classics at Merchant Taylors' Boys School in the 1940s.

Originally, the settlement on the banks of the Mersey which developed into Liverpool was a berewick (subsidiary farm) of the old Saxon manor at West Derby. Garston also started life as a berewick of the same manor.

Lord Street, now the centre of Liverpool's shopping area, used to be an orchard serving the castle which stood where the Victoria Monument now stands.

Copperas Hill, which runs alongside the Adelphi Hotel, takes its name from the old word for copper sulphate. There used to

How Copperas Hill looked in the eighteenth and nineteenth centuries.

be a factory on the site which produced 'copperas' but the locals had it removed in 1756 because of the foul smells involved in the production process.

Most people (even non-Welsh speakers) will have heard of the *Eisteddfod* held in Llangollen every year. But there is such a strong Welsh connection with Liverpool that these festivals of Welsh music and poetry were held in Liverpool in 1884, 1900 and 1929. In 1879 and 1917 the festival was held in Birkenhead.

In the village of Hale, near Speke, there is a very special gravestone. According to the epitaph the remains beneath are those of one John Middleton (1578–1623) known as 'the Childe of Hale' who was reputed to have been 9ft 3in tall. His portrait can still be seen in Brasenose College, Oxford. Not to be confused with 'child', the word 'childe' is archaic for a youth of noble birth.

YAGAN'S HEAD

Stories about graveyards and cemeteries are normally fairly sombre but the tale of Yagan's head is even more gruesome than most. In 1997 a severed head was exhumed from Everton cemetery where it had lain in a rotting plywood box since 1964, and it has since become known simply as Yagan's head.

Yagan was a member of the Noongar people of south-western Australia and can rightly be considered as one of Australia's early freedom fighters. During some sort of confrontation with the white settlers, Yagan was shot dead. But instead of giving him a decent burial the settlers chopped off his head and shipped it back to England to be displayed in a museum for the fascination and entertainment of curious visitors. By 1964, however, the head had begun to rot and so it was decided to bury it and Everton cemetery was the spot chosen for the interment. By the 1980s the Noongar people were beginning to request the return of their noble ancestor's head and whereas no objections were raised by the authorities, certain religious and legal problems did arise. Yagan's head had been buried very close to where still-born babies and a couple who died shortly after birth were lying at peace. Permission from the infants' next of kin to disturb the bodies was difficult or impossible to obtain and so another solution had to be found. After geological and archaeological surveys had been carried out it was agreed that the head could be extracted by sinking a well nearby and boring horizontally until Yagan's partial grave could be located. Eventually the undertaking ended in success, the head was retrieved and handed over to a deputation of the Noongar people who took it back to Australia for a decent burial. After some dispute about burying the head without a body, it was finally laid to rest in July 2010.

THE WALTON BOGGART

Legend has it that Walton is haunted by a supernatural presence known as a 'boggart'. This is supposed to be the ghost of a young Irish colleen captured and brought to the Liverpool area by Richard, son of Gilbert de Walton, a favourite of King Henry II (r. 1154–89). Richard apparently was a wild, uncontrollable youth who got his kicks by indulging in the occasional bout of cruelty and sadism. The story goes that he tied this colleen's wrists to his stirrup and then set off at a gallop, yelling at her to run faster and faster to keep pace. Obviously she could not and she soon stumbled. This caused the horse to come crashing down, sending Richard head over heels into a ditch. He was not best pleased and to show his displeasure he took out his sword and hacked the poor girl to death. He then threw her body into a stream and rode away as fast as he could. In the modern version of the story, the girl reappears now and again in the Cherry Lane area to frighten the life out of the residents. And there are even those who connect the killing with the unexplained traffic accidents which have been reported in the area over the years.

SOME FAMOUS VISITORS TO LIVERPOOL

Colonel W.F. Cody, otherwise known as Buffalo Bill brought his 'Wild West Show' to Liverpool in 1891. A member of his troupe was Annie Oakley (born Phoebe Anne Oakley Mozee), known to most people for her role in *Annie Get Your Gun.*

Charles Dickens, who is recognised as probably England's finest novelist, visited Liverpool several times, the last being in 1869, just before his death in 1870. He enrolled as a special constable in Liverpool in order to get a feel for what it was like to live in a deprived urban area. His experiences provided material which he later used in his novels.

Daniel Defoe, the author of *Robinson Crusoe,* was a fairly frequent visitor between 1680 and 1715 and expressed his delight in how fine a city it was.

Herman Melville, the author of *Moby Dick,* visited Liverpool in 1839 and made reference to the Liver Bird in his novel *Redburn: His First Voyage* (1849).

Roy Rogers, the cowboy star of stage and screen in the 1940s and '50s, stayed in the Adelphi Hotel with his wife, Dale Evans, and their horse Trigger in 1954. According to newspaper reports of the time the horse was allowed to wander around the hotel with a minimum of supervision. Let's hope he was house trained!

Samuel L. Clemens, known to the world as Mark Twain, the author of *Huckleberry Finn*, stayed in Liverpool in the 1870s.

Theodore 'Teddy' Roosevelt came to Liverpool in May 1869 where he visited his uncle, James Dunwoody Bulloch, an American Confederate States naval officer who was acting as his country's agent to Great Britain at the time.

Eric Blair aka **George Orwell** visited Liverpool in 1936 when he was gathering material about the effects of unemployment for his book *The Road to Wigan Pier*.

The Lumière brothers, credited with inventing cinema photography, visited Liverpool in 1897 and made a film from the late lamented Overhead Railway, the world's first electrically powered elevated railway system.

Liverpool's Overhead Light Railway as it looked in the 1950s.

Bill Haley, one of the world's first rock'n'roll singers, performed at the Odeon cinema with his band (The Comets) in 1955.

Pope John Paul II visited Liverpool in 1982.

J.B. Priestley, the author and playwright, was a frequent visitor to Liverpool.

Bob Dylan, the American singer, performed live at the Odeon on Lime Street on 1 May 1965.

Boris Johnson, journalist and politician, travelled to Liverpool in October 2004 to apologise for undeservedly scurrilous remarks he had passed about Scousers in a an article in *The Spectator*.

Condoleezza Rice, the then-US Secretary of State, visited Liverpool in March 2006. During her time in the city she stayed at a hotel in Hope Street.

HRH the Prince of Wales visited the city in April 2007 when he opened the newly refurbished St George's Hall.

FAMOUS SCOUSERS' NAME CHANGES

Derek Acorah, TV personality, was born Derek Francis Johnson (1950).

Cilla Black, singer, was born Priscilla Maria Veronica White (1943).

Dixie Dean, footballer, was born William Ralph Dean (1907).

Les Dennis, comedian, was born Leslie Dennis Heseltine (1953).

Kenny Everett, comedian, was born Maurice James Christopher Cole (1944).

Billy Fury, pop singer, was born Ronald William Wycherley (1940).

Sir Rex Harrison, actor, was born Reginald Carey Harrison (1908).

Sharon Maughan, actress, was born Sharon Patricia Mughan (1950).

Freddie Starr, comedian, was born Frederick Leslie Fowell (1943).

Ringo Starr, drummer, was born Richard Starkey (1940).

Frankie Vaughan, singer, was born Frank Abelson (1928).

Lynda La Plante, playwright, was born Lynda J. Titchmarsh (1943).

Ian Hart, actor, was born Ian Davies (1964).

Cherie Blair, lawyer and wife of the former Prime Minister, was born Theresa Cara Booth (1954).

Ted Ray, comedian, was born Charlie Olden (1905).

Faith Brown, comedienne, was born Eunice Irene Carroll (1944).

Michael Holliday, singer, was born Norman Alexander Milne (1924)

Billy J. Kramer, singer, was born William Howard Ashton (1943).

Anne Ziegler, singer, was born Irené Frances Eastwood (1910).

TWIN CITIES

Liverpool is twinned with Cologne (Germany), Dublin (Republic of Ireland), Shanghai (China) and Rio de Janeiro (Brazil).

The city also has consular links with Hungary, Italy, The Netherlands, Norway, Sweden, Thailand and the Cape Verde Islands.

There are also so-called 'friendship links' with Givenchy-lès-la-Bassée (France), Halifax (Canada), Havana (Cuba), La Plata (Argentina), Memphis (USA), Minamitane (Japan), Naples (Italy), New Orleans(USA), Odessa (Ukraine), Ponsacco (Italy), Râmnicu Vâlcea (Romania) and Valparaíso (Chile).

LIVERPOOL HUMOUR: EXAMPLE FOUR

Yer couldn't punch an 'ole in a wet *Echo*
or
Yer couldn't lick the skin off a rice puddin'
You're too weak to even contemplate fighting me

DID YOU KNOW?

Liverpool was the first city to provide its school children with free meals at midday and a bottle of milk mid-morning.

In 2004 Liverpool was declared a World Heritage Site by UNESCO.

Everton cemetery is not in Everton; it is in Fazakerley which is situated about 3 miles north of Everton. And Kirkdale cemetery is not in Kirkdale; it is in Aintree, also about 3 miles north of where its name suggests it should be.

The clocks on the Royal Liver Building, each with a diameter of 25ft, are larger than those of Big Ben in London.

In about 1800 one of the most important industries in Liverpool was watchmaking. It has been estimated that at its height, the industry employed something in the region of 2,000 people.

Liverpool is sometimes referred to as 'The Capital of Wales'. No doubt this is because of the large Welsh population in the city and the ease with which people can and do travel from Wales to Liverpool to do their shopping.

The veteran Liverpool actor Geoffrey Hughes (*Coronation Street*, *Keeping up Appearances*, *Heartbeat*, etc.) was Deputy Lieutenant for the Isle of Wight (i.e. was the queen's representative on the island) from 2009 until his death at the age of 68 in July 2012.

Liverpool can lay claim to having scored a number of valuable firsts:

the first school for the blind
the first high school for girls
the first council house
the first juvenile court
the first lifeboat station
the first public baths and wash-houses
the first district nurse

IF YOU ARE A STRANGER TO LIVERPOOL YOU NEED TO KNOW THAT . . .

a moggy is	a cat
a jigger rabbit is	a stray cat
a bevy is	a drink
hen fruit is	an egg
depth charges are	oysters
black tapioca is	caviar
a scuffer is	a policeman
a judy-scuffer is	a policewoman
a meaty (meat wagon) is	a Black Maria
the rec (recreation ground) is	the park
this 'avvy is	this afternoon
an 'ozzie is	a hospital
a boxer is	an undertaker
Irish confetti are	stone chippings
A bone orchard is	a cemetery
A glass of Corpy pop is	a glass of water
Ar (our) kid	my brother
Cum (come) 'ed	either 'come here' or 'hurry up'

You might also hear phrases such as . . .

'Is 'ead's as big as Birkenhead: he is rather over-confident
'E stands around like one of Lewis's: he watches while everyone else works
'E's a left-footer: he is an adherent of the Roman Catholic faith
'E's a Proddy dog: he is an adherent of the Protestant faith
Me dogs are barking: I have very sore feet
She's a docker with lippy on: that lady is not very attractive
'Er ring's in the Mountains o' Morn: she's pawned her ring
Ta, la (pron: tar lar): thank you, sir
I'm dead made up: I am very pleased, delighted
I'm dead chuffed: I am very happy
'E could wind the Liver clock: he's very tall
She's got a gob like a parish oven: that lady is rather talkative
'E's out chuckin' arrers: He's gone for a game of darts
Dat's dead gear, darris: That looks excellent to me

She's in Dickie's meadow now: she's in trouble/in a bit of a fix

D'ya wanna a dekko at this?: Would you care to examine this more closely?

D'yanowarrameanlike?: Have you fully understood what I am saying?

And if you are asked any of these questions you are being threatened:

Like wakin' up widda crowd around ya, do ya?

Like 'ozzie (hospital) food, do ya?

You talkin' to me or chewin' a brick?

On the other hand, these are an indication that the speaker wishes you well:

I 'ope you get to 'eaven 'alf an hour before the devil knows yer dead.

Good night, and may ya see yer toes in the mornin'.

(These expressions are both thought to be Irish in origin.)

Don't confuse the following:

'ozzie – hospital

crozzie - cross-bar (also a ride on the cross-bar)

cozzie – bathing costume, swimming trunks

'cos 'e – because he

So you might hear, 'Ar kid's in de 'ozzie 'cos 'e fell off a crozzie when 'e was only wearin' a cozzie.'

'My brother is in hospital because he fell off the cross-bar on a bicycle when he was only wearing a pair of swimming trunks.'

LIVERPOOL HUMOUR: EXAMPLE FIVE

There's nothin' in 'ere worth puttin' me specs on for

So far I haven't seen anything I like in this shop

DID YOU KNOW?

New Brighton, just over the river from Liverpool, once had its own tower. It was modelled on the Eiffel Tower in Paris and was something of a rival to Britain's only other tower in Blackpool. The New Brighton version was completed in 1900 and stood 567ft (Blackpool's opened in 1894 and was 518ft tall). Unfortunately it had a very short shelf life: it was closed during the First World War and dismantled in about 1920.

The first large-scale railway tunnel under water was hollowed out under the Mersey between 1883 and 1886. The Prince of Wales declared the line open at a ceremony held at James Street station. For the first few years the engines ran on steam and then the line was electrified in 1903.

During the Second World War the people of Liverpool were defended by no less a person than the future Prime Minister of Great Britain. Sir Edward Heath, then a second lieutenant in the Artillery Regiment, was posted in 1941 to the Chester 107 Heavy Anti-Aircraft Regiment which was part of the defences against enemy planes coming in to bomb Liverpool.

Pope Benedict did not visit Liverpool during his visit to Great Britain in September 2010.

In Liverpool, and much of the surrounding area, the festival everybody else calls Christmas is referred to as 'Crimbo'. 'Daddy Crimbo' is the venerable gentleman the rest of the country calls Father Christmas or Santa Claus.

One of the Three Graces at the Pier Head, the Cunard Building, is named after Sir Samuel Cunard (1787–1865) who was born in Canada (Nova Scotia) and came to England and set up his transatlantic steamship company in Liverpool in 1840.

Liverpool John Moores University has a music legend for a Chancellor – Dr Brian May of the group Queen was installed in April 2008.

LIVERPOOL IS NOT ALONE!

There is also:
Liverpool in Nova Scotia, Canada
Liverpool in the Brazilian jungle
Liverpool in New York State, USA
Liverpool in Pennsylvania, USA
Liverpool in Illinois, USA
Liverpool in Texas, USA
Liverpool in New South Wales, Australia

and there's:
Garston in Hertfordshire
Everton in Bedfordshire

Downtown Liverpool . . . Texas, USA.

Everton in Arkansas and Missouri (USA)

Warrington in Milton Keynes, two in Pennsylvania, one in Florida (USA)

Walton in Somerset, Surrey, Suffolk, Peterborough, Leicestershire and Cumbria

Bootle in Cumbria

Dingle in County Kerry, Ireland

Crosby in Lincolnshire, Isle of Man and in the USA there is a Crosby in each of: North Dakota, Minnesota, Arkansas, Mississippi and Texas, while there is also a Crosby in Ontario, Canada

Waterloo in Belgium

Netherton in Worcestershire

Kirkby in Nottinghamshire and Lincolnshire

LIVERPOOL HUMOUR: EXAMPLE SIX

She's got a gob on 'er like the Mersey Tunnel
She can be quite loquacious at times

DID YOU KNOW?

During the 1950s and '60s if a little girl broke her dolly she could take it to the Dolls' Hospital situated next door to the YMCA on Mount Pleasant where it could stay until it was feeling better (i.e. repaired). It is now on Smithdown Road.

Dick Turpin, the famous eighteenth-century highwayman, is reputed to have spent time with his horse Black Bess in Hunt's Cross when he was on his way to York.

Thomas De Quincy, the author of *Confessions of an English Opium Eater* (1821) lived for some time in Everton in the early part of the nineteenth century.

In Liverpool old people are often referred to as 'twerlies'. This is simply because they were born 'too early'.

St Andrew's graveyard with its unusual final resting place.

CERTAINLY ECCENTRIC
AND PROBABLY UNIQUE

If you are the kind of person who likes wandering around graveyards reading the epitaphs, on your next visit to Liverpool you should head for St Andrew's Church in Rodney Street. The church is now all boarded up, but at the side and quite visible from the road is a monument in the shape of a pyramid. There are at least two explanations for this rather strange graveyard adornment. The first is that a certain James Mackenzie, a railway employee, was a devotee of the gaming tables and expressed the wish that, after his death, he should be buried sitting at a table holding a winning hand of cards. His friends remembered his wishes and, when he died, sat him at a table inside the pyramid which is still there today. The other explanation is that James is in the pyramid in a standing position as he believed that this way the devil would be unable to claim his soul. The pyramid was erected in 1868.

DID YOU KNOW?

A dog butty is a sandwich comprised of a slice of corned beef between two slices of bread. And in a Welsh butty the filling is a slice of cheese with a few rings of raw onion.

On 18 November 1983 Graham and Janet Walton of Liverpool had bit of a shock. They became the proud parents of the world's first set of girl sextuplets who survived. The girls (Hannah, Sarah, Luci, Ruth, Jennifer and Kate) were born in Liverpool Women's Hospital.

William Brown Street used to be called Shaw's Brow.

Lime Street was originally Lime Kiln Lane because it was lined on one side with lime kilns.

FANCY TRYING SOME SCOUSE?

The original ingredients of 'scouse', introduced by Scandinavian sailors, were meat, potatoes, carrots and ship's biscuits. In the bad old days if a poor family in Liverpool was even more strapped for cash than usual this cheap culinary delicacy could be made even cheaper by leaving the meat out. Then the meal that appeared on the table was known as 'blind scouse'. And 'dead scouse' is a plate of the delicacy that's been allowed to go cold. There are many recipes for 'scouse' and they all claim to be the original. Modern recipes include all sorts of exotic ingredients such as olive oil, thyme and Worcester sauce, few of which would have ever been heard of in a working-class Liverpool house not so many years ago. So if you want to try the ordinary scouse produced by working class mothers trying to feed their families 50 or 60 years ago, try this one.

Ingredients (amounts are just approximations)

half a pound of lamb or beef	1 or 2 Oxo cubes
a large onion	salt and pepper
1lb carrots	water
5lbs potatoes	

Method

Cut the meat into fairly large cubes and fry in lard or dripping until they are a nice golden brown colour (I suppose modern cooks will prefer vegetable oil, but for authenticity it has to be lard or dripping).

Now transfer the meat to a saucepan, peel and chop the carrots, onion and potatoes into rustic, chunky cubes. Add the carrots, onions and half the potatoes to the pan, cover with water and add the stock, salt and pepper.

Now put the pan on the hob and bring everything to the boil. Once the water is boiling turn the heat down and let everything simmer away for about two hours, giving it a gentle stir every now and then. After the two hours add the remainder of the potatoes and allow it all to simmer for another hour or two (depending on taste).

When ready, serve the scouse on warm plates with a good helping of pickled beetroot, red cabbage or pickled onions. There should be enough with this recipe for between four and six people.

For a slight variant on the above, you might like to try serving the scouse directly onto a thick slice of bread. It's a bit stodgy, but delicious and just the thing to keep you warm on a cold winter's night.

LIVERPOOL HUMOUR: EXAMPLE SEVEN

'E's just bought himself a new Toxteth briefcase
He has bought himself a new portable stereo

DID YOU KNOW?

Before the introduction of All Figure Dialling (AFD) in 1966 telephone numbers were made up of three letters plus the number (usually four digits). A classic case is often heard in old British detective films when the number for the police at Scotland Yard in London is given as Whitehall 1212. Dialling the number a caller would have dialled **WHI** 1212. In and around Liverpool the exchanges included: **CEN**tral, **NOR**th, **AIN**tree, **ARG**osy, **ROY**al, **MAG**hull, **HUN**t's Cross, **STO**neycroft, **WAL**ton, **LAR**k Lane, **ALL**erton, **CRO**sby, **WAT**erloo **BRO**ad Green, **TUE**brook, **HUY**ton. Before AFD the telephone number for The Cavern was **CEN**tral 1591.

Liverpool used to have 'pugs'. These were specially designed little trains which shunted up and down in industrial and dock areas of the country and were frequently used in places where space was at a premium. Officially (and this is for the train-spotters!) they were locomotives of the L&YR Class 21 0–4–0ST type and could be seen puffing along on 4ft 8½in gauge track in front of the Three Graces up to the late 1950s.

In Liverpool a 'Woollyback' is anybody who comes from Lancashire, particularly towns such as Wigan and St Helens.

The poet and illustrator Edward Lear (1812–88), known to all for such nonsense rhymes as *The Owl and the Pussycat*, was employed by the Earl of Derby in 1832 to produce drawings of the parrots in his private menagerie at Knowsley Hall, just outside Liverpool.

On Ormskirk Road near to the Old Roan pub there is a very odd-looking building. It is now just the remaining tower of a once much larger edifice, crowned with mobile phone aerials and has the word PARADOX (this is all that remains from the time when the building was home to the Paradox night club) writ large on all four sides. In a previous incarnation this was the home of Vernons Pools but it is many a long year since the girls checked the pools forms in this building looking for the week's winner. Less well known, however, is the fact that this building was taken over by MI5 during the Second World War for highly secret intelligence work.

'Ye Hole in Ye Wall' in Hackin's Hey claims to be the oldest pub in the city as it dates back to 1726. But 'The Slaughterhouse' in Fenwick Street also lays claim to the title.

Emma Hamilton, the mistress of Horatio Nelson, was born on the Wirral in 1765.

How many people who
walk under this sign know
what it really says? Inside
this pub the 'ladies' and
'gents' signs are written in
Irish: mná and fir.

The pub on Seel Street known as Pogue Mahone's is a joke. It's
really just how the Irish Gaelic *póg mo thón* is pronounced and
means 'kiss my bum'.

The very first bowling green in Liverpool was laid out in the
grounds of the Black Horse pub near Walton church. At the time
the pub was called the White Horse.

Liverpool's first purpose-built cinema was the Bedford in Bedford
Road, Walton. It was opened on 26 December 1908.

The world has a Liverpudlian to thank for the crossword puzzle! The very first one appeared in the *New York World* on 21 December 1913 and was compiled by Arthur Wynne (1871–1945), who lived most of his life in America but was born in Liverpool.

The world's first pet shop was opened in Liverpool in 1872.

From 1793 to 1796 Liverpool suffered a financial crisis which meant that many of the town's merchants and businessmen went bankrupt. One consequence of the crash was that, for a while, Liverpool printed its own banknotes.

Liverpool's famous Playhouse Theatre was originally known as The Star Music Hall.

Central Park, New York, was modelled on Birkenhead Park.

Europe's first tram service began operation in Birkenhead in 1860 and, believe it or not, its creator rejoiced in the name of George Francis Train. Birkenhead's last tram ran in 1937.

In 1896 Sir W.P. Hartley, famed for his jam factory in Walton, donated the clock for the Jubilee Tower which forms part of the University of Liverpool buildings.

When the Grand National was held on 26 March 1955 a punter could travel to the course from Dingle in south Liverpool to Aintree station near the racecourse for 2s return (10p in today's money).

It seems odd now, but in the early years of the nineteenth century Liverpool was famed for its bathing beach. The 'North Shore' as it was known, stretched all the way from Chapel Street to the sand hills at Seaforth, a distance of about 4 miles. It was a popular spot for people who had discovered the pleasure and health benefits to be had from bathing in the sea.

Brigadier Sir Philip Toosey (1904–75) was a much decorated soldier in the British Army in the Second World War. He was born in Birkenhead and commanded 236 Battery of the Territorial Army, based in Aigburth, in the 1930s. He is best remembered, however, as the officer in charge of building the famous (and infamous) bridge over the River Kwai, immortalised in film with Toosey played on screen by Sir Alec Guinness (although in the film his name was changed to Col. Nicholson). When the film was first shown it appalled many of the men who served under him as it seemed to suggest that he had collaborated with the enemy.

One of the world's first Christmas grottos was opened in the Bon Marché department store on Liverpool's Church Street in 1879.

THE KING (AKA THE MOLE) OF EDGEHILL

Back in the eighteenth century there was a man by the name of Joseph Williamson (b. 1769) who was, to say the least, a bit of an oddball. Almost nothing is known of his early life but he showed up in Liverpool in 1780 looking for work. In a typical 'rags-to-riches' career he went from wandering the streets looking for work to finding a job and then marrying well and living the rest of his life in comfort. But he had a bit of a thing about digging holes; not just the odd hole in his back garden, but deep vaults under the ground around Edge Hill. He employed gangs of labourers to dig cavernous tunnels with supporting archways in a series of subterranean labyrinths. But the magnificent engineering feat appears to have had no purpose. It has been suggested that Williamson just wanted to keep the men, who would otherwise have been unemployed, occupied, but we simply do not know. He never divulged his reasoning and nobody has been able to offer more than an uneducated guess to explain his activities. Perhaps he was mad, perhaps just eccentric; but his 'hobby' earned him the nickname 'The King of Edgehill'. Today some of the 'King's' tunnels have been filled in and lie under commercial buildings not far from the city centre, but most have been opened to the public.

2

HOW IT ALL BEGAN

A LIVERPOOL HISTORY TIMELINE

3000 BC	Early settlements known to have existed around Calderstones.
AD 43–5th century	Evidence of Roman settlements have been found at Chester and places such as Garston and Woolton.
c. **AD 900**	Vikings settled along both sides of the Mersey.
1207	King John founded the port of Liverpool to transport men and supplies to Ireland. Original town consisted of seven streets. First Charter granted.
1229	King Henry III granted Liverpool another charter. Merchants now had the right to form their own guilds.
1235	By now a castle looked over the town.
1295	Liverpool was given permission to send two MPs to parliament.
1351	William, son of Adam, was Liverpool's first mayor. The town also now held weekly markets and annual fairs.
1515	A grammar school, attached to the church of St Mary del Key was founded in Liverpool.

1558	The first of many plagues struck Liverpool.
1600	The population of Liverpool was now thought to be about 2,000.
1644	Liverpool fell to the Royalists for a brief time during the Civil War.
1700	The population of Liverpool reaches approximately 5,000.
1704	St Peter's Parish Church was built in what is now Church Street.
1708	A Bluecoat school was built for the sons of the poor.
1715	Liverpool's first dock was completed.
c. **1730**	Liverpool merchants involved in the African slave trade.
1748	Watchmen were appointed to patrol the streets at night.
1749	Foundation of Liverpool Royal Infirmary.
1754	A new Town Hall was built.
1778	A dispensary where the poor could obtain free medicines was opened.
1801	Liverpool's population now about 77,000.
1830	Horse-drawn buses began operating in Liverpool.
1849	Philharmonic Hall built.
1852	Central Library built.

1857	Municipal water supply commenced.
1865	First horse-drawn trams begin operating.
1870	Stanley Park opened for the benefit of the public.
1872	Sefton Park opened.
1877	Opening of Walker Art Gallery.
1879	Opening of Picton Reading Room.
1898–1901	Trams converted to run on electricity.
1908	Tower Building built.
1911	Liver Building built.
1916	Building of the Cunard offices.
1928	A survey revealed that 14 per cent of Liverpool's population lived in poverty.
1934	Opening to traffic of the Queensway Tunnel.
1967	Consecration of the Catholic cathedral.

1971	New tunnel, the Kingsway, was built.
1978	Completion of the Anglican cathedral.
1980	Opening of the Merseyside Maritime Museum.
1981	Riots in Toxteth.
1980s	Redevelopment of the Albert Dock.
1988	Tate Gallery of Modern Art opened.
1993	Museum of Liverpool Life opened.
1996	Opening of the Institute for Performing Arts.
2008	Liverpool was the European Capital of Culture.
2010	Lewis's department store closes after 155 years.

LIVERPOOL HUMOUR: EXAMPLE EIGHT

Don't dirty the table cloth, yer dad hasn't read it yet
Overheard in a docker's house in the 1960s

LIVERPOOL'S HISTORY –
A POTTED VERSION

c. AD *900*
The Norsemen began arriving from Scandinavia and settled along both sides of the Mersey. Evidence of their existence can still be seen today in the Norse place names that survive all over the area: Crosby, Meols, Neston, Kirkby, Thingwall, Thurstaston, Toxteth, Aigburth, Litherland and many more.

1086
Places such as West Derby, Toxteth and Speke appeared in the Domesday Book, but there was no mention of Liverpool.

1190

The name 'Liverpul' was mentioned in papers signed by King John. This is taken to mean 'muddy pool' but the linguistic basis for such an interpretation is shaky. An alternative spelling from about the same time, Litherpool, might provide a better clue. 'Lither' is derived from an Old Norse word meaning 'slope' and so 'slope down to the pool' or 'pool near the slope' could be a more likely origin of the name.

1207

King John decided to create a borough out of the fishing village we now know as Liverpool. The first streets which made up the new town were Bank Street (now Water Street), Chapel Street, Juggler Street (now High Street), Whiteacre Street (now Old Hall Street), Dale Street and Moor Street (now Tithebarn Street). Castle Street is thought to have been added later. History tells us that his main purpose for developing Liverpool was that he wanted a secure harbour for his navy which would carry troops over to Ireland.

1235

The Sherriff of Lancaster, William de Ferrers, took charge of the later stages of building Liverpool's castle. It occupied the site where the Victoria Monument stands just outside the Law Courts. At one time it

The old castle on the site now occupied by the Victoria Monument.

was the residence of the Molyneux family but for much of its long life it remained virtually unoccupied and unused. It was demolished in 1726.

1315
Thomas of Lancaster, then occupant of the castle, rebelled against King Edward II. The outcome was a bit of a disaster for Thomas, not least because his actions lead to the castle being attacked.

1346
The town how had almost 200 burgesses and was beginning to develop as a commercial centre. The population was thought to have been about 1,000 by this time.

1349–50
The plague known generally as the Black Death struck Liverpool several times. Many people died and the graveyards were unable to cope.

1355
The construction of St Nicholas's Church began close to the water's edge. Originally the site was occupied by a small chapel called St Mary del Key.

1406
Sir John Stanley was given royal permission to enlarge and fortify his house at the water's edge. The house eventually developed into what we now know as the Tower, occupied for centuries by the powerful Stanley family.

1424
The two rival Liverpool dynasties, the Molyneux and Stanley families, almost came to blows on the streets of the burgeoning town. Nobody knows exactly what the quarrel was about and, in all probability, was nothing more than a power struggle to determine which family should be the dominant one in the area.

1485
Thomas Stanley was made Earl of Derby by Henry Tudor in exchange for the support he gave him at the Battle of Bosworth (24 August) during the War of the Roses.

1530

By this date Liverpool had acquired paved streets. We know this from the account of a visit made by John Leland, the London-born poet and antiquary frequently credited with being the father of English local history.

1558

Another outbreak of the plague reduced Liverpool's population by about a third. The population numbers had not recovered from the earlier plagues and so, after this most recent visitation, was now no more than a few hundred.

1586

Liverpool overtook Chester as the most prosperous and important port in England's north-west. There were probably several factors at work here, but the most important was the silting-up of the River Dee.

1601

As a commercial port, Liverpool's expansion continued apace mainly because of increasing trade with Ireland and the expansion of Lancashire's textile industry.

1604

The area known as Toxteth Park, once a hunting ground used by King John, was sold to the Molyneux family who turned it into arable land and pasture.

1642–4

The Civil War raged throughout England and Liverpool changed hands several times, now occupied by the Royalists, now by the Parliamentarians.

1667

The ship *The Antelope* returned from Barbados with a cargo of sugar and immediately Liverpool's fate for the next 300-odd years was sealed. Sugar imports (and later sugar refining) became one of the major industries of the town.

1699

William III made Liverpool an independent parish for the first time in its history.

1700

A new century and a new (and shameful) trade began to make some people in Liverpool very rich. The new commerce was slavery, frequently referred to euphemistically as the 'African trade'. Very few, if any slaves actually set foot in Liverpool, but there were shops in the town that sold implements of torture and/or restraint which ships' captains could use if their 'passengers' caused them any problems. By the 1760s Liverpool was the country's leading slave trading port and in 1799 it accounted for no fewer than 45,000 slaves being transported from Africa to the Americas.

1709–15

The engineers moved in and Liverpool became the first port in the world to acquire a wet dock. It occupied a position at the mouth of the 'pool' and is both an enormous undertaking and a remarkable achievement. By the time the dock was completed it could accommodate up to 100 ships.

1716–18

The building and then the official opening of the Bluecoat Hospital and school took place in which the retired sea captain Bryan Blundell gave shelter to the children of the poor. The building is still on its original site today, in School Lane, just behind Church Street.

1737–54

The first wet dock (completed in 1715) was so successful that the authorities decided to build another. This was constructed between 1734 and 1753 and is the dock we know today as the Salthouse Dock.

1775

The American War of Independence caused a recession in Liverpool. The seamen suffered a loss of income, rioted in the streets and even attacked the Town Hall.

1790

Business now boomed as imports of raw cotton from the West Indies soared. The textile industry in Lancashire expanded dramatically and Liverpool reaped much of the benefit.

1790s

Liverpool developed a conscience! Notable figures such Dr James Currie, William Roscoe, William Rathbone *et al.* begin to speak out against the inhumane trade of slavery. At first the movement was ignored but then gradually started to win adherents.

1807

After a long campaign the anti-slavery movement won and slavery was abolished throughout the British colonies. Many thought that Liverpool would die as a port when the 'African trade' dried up but they were proven overly pessimistic. Cotton imports more than compensated for the loss.

1808

Merchants and traders spotted the increasing need for low-cost housing in and around the docks caused by the boom in trade. High-density accommodation sprang up, particularly of the type centred around a 'court' which was soon to become characteristic of the slum dwellings for which Liverpool became famous.

1813
The British government decided to end the East India Company's monopoly on trade with India and China, and Liverpool was not slow to take advantage of the opening up of new trade routes.

1824
Great expansion of the wet dock system under the stewardship of Jesse Hartley began. Eventually it spread over 140 acres of extra dock space to accommodate the ever-increasing demands on shipping.

1825
The institution which developed into what we now know as the Liverpool John Moores University was founded. The Mechanics' Institute was opened and later went through several reincarnations: the College of Commerce, the Liverpool Polytechnic and finally LJMU.

1826
The first sod was dug signalling the start to laying the railway line between Liverpool and Manchester. Under the guidance of George Stephenson the line took four years to build but, when finished, was the world's first passenger railway.

1832
Liverpool was hit by an epidemic of cholera which infected almost 5,000 people, of whom over 1,500 died. Almost certainly the outbreak was due to the unsanitary living conditions endured by most of the population. Little was done to improve these conditions and cholera revisited the town no fewer than three more times before the end of the century.

1835
Liverpool was designated as an Assize Town, meaning that it now had the right to create its own Law Courts. The decision was instrumental in the design and building of St George's Hall in 1854, which was partly used for entertainment and partly as courts of law.

1840
The Canadian Samuel Cunard came to Liverpool and established his shipping line, operating a twice-monthly service across the Atlantic.

1844–50
The population of Liverpool was now greatly increased due to the thousands of Irish men and women who flooded into the town. The potato blight had caused famine in Ireland and many left in desperation, searching for food and accommodation in an already overcrowded Liverpool.

1850
The company known as the Royal Liver Assurance was founded in Liverpool, now probably one of the most important centres for the insurance industry in the country.

1856
The first department store in Liverpool was opened by David Lewis. It burned down once, was bombed in the Second World War (rebuilt in 1952) but finally closed for business in June 2010.

1857
The daily running of the port is taken out of the hands of the Corporation and handed over to a new body, the Mersey Docks and Harbour Board.

1860
The William Brown Library and Museum was opened to the public.

1868
Liverpool was the first borough to be granted permission by Act of Parliament to operate a tram system for the benefit of its citizens.

1872
Sugar from the West Indies was now refined in Mr Tate's factory in Love Lane. The factory remained in operation for just over 100 years but was closed down by the EEC planners in Brussels as they preferred to aid the sugar beet industry in East Anglia.

1878
Everton Football Club was born. It was originally just a boys' club football team from St Domingo's Methodist Church in Everton but someone decided that it was time to put their weekend kickabouts onto a more formal footing. Right from the start the team was referred to as 'the toffees' because of their association with a part of Liverpool famed for its toffee making.

1880
Liverpool became a city.

1881
The University of Liverpool was founded by royal charter. It was originally designated a university college and was built on the site of a former lunatic asylum in Brownlow Hill. It is still there today.

1885
The huge Irish electorate in the Scotland Road area of the town chose a Sinn Féin candidate, T.P. O'Connor, to represent it at Westminster.

1886
An underground railway link between Liverpool and Birkenhead was opened.

1890
Pogroms in Russia caused an influx of Russian Jews to move into Liverpool.

1892
An important year in the history of football. Everton FC took up residence in Goodison, following a dispute over rent with the team's landlords. In the same year the team that was to become Everton's rival in the city, Liverpool FC, was formed.

1893
Liverpool now had the authority to appoint a Lord Mayor. In the same year the Overhead Railway opened and served the docks for the next 50 years.

1895
Toxteth, Wavertree, Walton and West Derby all became part of the municipality of Liverpool.

1902
Garston was also absorbed into the Liverpool borough.

1904
Sir Giles Gilbert Scott saw his dream taking shape as the Anglican cathedral began to redefine the Liverpool skyline.

1905
Fazakerley, lying 6 or 7 miles to the north of the city centre, was swallowed up and became another Liverpool suburb.

1907–16
Liverpool's shoreline was completely reshaped as an artificial island was created at the bottom of Bank Street. The 'Pier Head', as it came to be known, had a completely new landing stage and acquired the now iconic buildings: the Cunard Building, the Royal

Liver Building and the office of the Mersey Docks and Harbour Board.

1909

Liverpool's reputation as a melting pot of nations where people from all over the world live in (more or less) perfect harmony was somewhat dented. Riots broke out in what was nothing less than an eruption of sectarian intolerance.

1911

The threat of revolution raised its ugly head in Liverpool. Transport workers went on strike and the government, fearing widespread insurrection, sent gunboats up the Mersey.

1919

More riots broke out which were rooted in the increasing racial tension developing in the city. At the same time the police went on strike, demanding increased wages, and many shops were looted.

1922

The increased prosperity Liverpool experienced briefly after the First World War came to an end and unemployment rose steeply. Unemployed males accounted for 20 per cent of the adult population and there was no noticeable improvement in the situation until the outbreak of the Second World War.

1925–34

Construction of the Mersey Tunnel (officially the Queensway Tunnel) between Liverpool and Birkenhead took place.

1929

The Wall Street Crash had a terrible effect on Liverpool. Ships lay idle in the docks and unemployment soared. Official records state that 30 per cent of the population were living below the poverty line and another 14 per cent just above it. These are the bald statistics; the reality is that most of the people in the city were experiencing extreme hardship and were surviving on what were little more than starvation rations.

1934

Littlewoods, based in Liverpool, introduced mail-order shopping. This was the first time such an innovation to the nation's shopping habits had been seen in Britain.

1936

Liverpool Council began a rapid building programme to house the ever-expanding population. Housing estates sprung up in Aintree, Kirkby and Speke.

1939

For some reason known only to themselves, the IRA (Irish Republican Army) blew up the swing bridge on the canal at Green Lane, Maghull. As the bridge was of no military significance whatsoever, the whole exercise seems to have been a waste of time and explosives.

1939–45

The country was at war with Germany and Liverpool was virtually a front-line city. It also became the nerve centre for operations in the Battle of the Atlantic.

1941

For the people of Liverpool this was probably the worst year in the whole history of the city. In May, the Luftwaffe bombers came over night after night and tried to wipe the city off the face of the earth. Thousands of bombs were dropped on the city centre and the suburbs, causing massive damage and killing almost 4,000 people while 70,000 were left homeless.

1945

The end of the war in Europe came about and the city celebrated. The only question at the back of people's minds was how long Japan would hold out. By August Japan too had surrendered and Liverpool started the long process of post-war recovery.

1950s

The government in London gave Liverpool priority for industrial regeneration after the war. Industries were encouraged to set up shop in or around the city in an effort to solve or at least alleviate the social problems associated with unemployment.

1952
The once tiny village of Kirkby (mentioned in the Domesday Book) was earmarked by the central government for expansion. A huge building programme got under way in order to solve the housing problem exacerbated by bombing during the war.

1956
The Overhead Railway succumbed to the ravages of salt and wind blown in off the Irish Sea. The structure was declared unsafe and too costly to repair and plans were drawn up for dismantling it.

1957
John Lennon made his first tentative steps into the music world by creating The Quarrymen. The name is taken from his school, Quarry Bank, one of Liverpool's long established grammar schools.

1962–7
The car manufacturing giants Vauxhall, Standard-Triumph and Ford set up factories near Halewood on the outskirts of Liverpool. Together they employed over 30,000 people.

1967
The Catholic cathedral was completed. It had been begun in the 1930s but building was suspended during hostilities and then resumed in 1962. Its revolutionary design meant that it was soon nicknamed 'Paddy's Wigwam' and 'The Mersey Funnel'.

1968
Roger McGough, Brian Patten and Adrian Henri, otherwise known as the 'Liverpool Poets', had their work officially recognised by the literary world when their anthology *Mersey Sound* was published by Penguin.

1971
The second Mersey Tunnel, officially designated the Kingsway Tunnel, was opened linking Liverpool to Wallasey. At the same time the revolutionary means of transporting vast amounts of freight by containerisation was introduced. Much of the work on the docks was streamlined and thousands of dockers were made redundant.

1978–85

Economically speaking, this was a dreadful time for the citizens of Liverpool. The manufacturing industries of the whole country contracted and in Liverpool factories closed by the dozen. At one point a quarter of the workforce was made redundant and the city began to look like a ghost-town. The feeling in the city was that London had abandoned it and the Thatcher government seemed unable or unwilling to tackle the problem and only decided to act after serious rioting spewed out onto the streets. Toxteth was particularly badly hit as riots, some of them economically and some racially motivated, caused thousands of pounds worth of damage and a policeman was killed.

1983–7

Soviet Russia almost came to the banks of the Mersey. The Tory government under Margaret Thatcher was seen as far too right-wing for the majority of Liverpudlians, particularly those in 'Thatcher's Army' i.e. the people who, through no fault of their own, found themselves on the dole. In such a political atmosphere, Trotskyite philosophy flourished and the extremely left-wing leader of the Militant Tendency, Derek Hatton, took over the running of the Council.

1988

Many people couldn't believe it, but in the midst of what teetered on the edge of social and economic breakdown, it was decided to open the Liverpool branch of London's art gallery, the Tate. When there had been rioting, near revolution, genuine hardship and people had left the city in their droves, an art gallery was not very high on most people's list of priorities.

2003

Liverpool was nominated as the Capital of Culture for the year 2008. Preparations commenced immediately and the city was swept by renewed feelings of pride as people put the recent troubles behind them.

2004
With an enormous grant from the EU the area around Paradise Street was earmarked for regeneration. The old, run-down part of the city was to be completely razed to the ground to make way for a total architectural overhaul.

2008
The whole world seemed to be gripped with enthusiasm for celebrating Liverpool as the European Capital of Culture. The resurrected area around Paradise Street (now known as Liverpool One) was a total triumph.

2010
Fans couldn't believe what they were hearing, but Liverpool FC was sold to the America-based group 'New England Sports Ventures'.

DID YOU KNOW?

CS gas was used for riot control for the first time on the British mainland in the Toxteth riots of the 1980s.

One of the last two people to be executed in Britain was Peter Allen. He was hanged in Walton Prison on 13 August 1964.

Kirkby was used for the pilot scheme for replacing foot patrols by panda cars for the police throughout Britain.

Hovis, Natwest, Ladbrokes and Coca-Cola have all commissioned adverts which were set in Liverpool.

3

IN AND AROUND LIVERPOOL

THE RIVER MERSEY

There is no getting away from the fact that without the River Mersey Liverpool would not exist. A town or city of a different kind might occupy the site, but its history, character and purpose would be entirely different from those enjoyed by the mighty port we have today.

Some basic facts about the Mersey:
Length: approximately 70 miles.
Source: the confluence of the rivers Goyt and Tame near Stockport. The rivers Gowy, Weaver, Bollin, Irwell, Etherow, Red Brook, Glaze Brook and Chorlton Brook are also tributaries.
Name: the derivation of the name is Anglo-Saxon and means 'border water'.

Tides: The river's tidal range is second only to that of the River Severn. It ranges from 13ft (approx.) neap tide to 33ft (approx.) Spring tide.

LIVERPOOL

Definition: Officially Liverpool is both a city and a metropolitan borough of Merseyside.
Population: 435,000 approx. (borough and city)

For local elections the area is divided into 30 council wards: Allerton and Hunt's Cross, Anfield, Belle Vale, Central, Childwall,

Church, Clubmoor, County, Cressington, Croxteth, Everton, Fazakerley, Greenbank, Kensington and Fairfield, Kirkdale, Knotty Ash, Mossley Hill, Norris Green, Old Swan, Picton, Prince's Park, Riverside, Speke Garston, St Michael's, Tuebrook and Stoneycroft, Warbreck, Wavertree, West Derby, Woolton and Yew Tree.

Liverpool has the oldest African community in Britain and is also home to the oldest Chinese community in the whole of Europe.

AROUND THE DISTRICTS

Aintree
Distance from centre: 6.5 miles
Population: 7, 200 (approx.)
Name origin: the Anglo-Saxon for 'one tree' or 'lone tree'.

The tree in question is thought to have stood in Bull Bridge Lane, one of the oldest parts of the village. It was taken down in 2004, despite local protests, because it had become diseased. Aintree is most famous for its racecourse which attracts visitors from all over the world.

Fazakerley
Distance from centre: 5 miles (approx.)
Population: 15,000 (approx.)
Name origin: from the Anglo-Saxon *faes* (edge), *aecer* (field) *lea* (clearing) so originally meant something like 'glade near the edge of the field.'

The Everton and England footballer Stuart Barlow was born in Fazakerley in 1968 while the Royal Ordnance Factory which used to be in Fazakerley was where the Lee-Enfield rifle, the Sterling and Sten submachine guns were produced for a while after the end of the Second World War.

Childwall

Distance from centre: 4 miles (approx.)
Population: 14,000 (approx.)
Name origin: appears in the Domesday Book as 'Cileuuelle' from the Anglo-Saxon *cild* 'youth' and *wella* 'stream', 'well' suggesting that it was a well where the youth of the area were in the habit of gathering.

Childwall is one of the most affluent areas of Liverpool and the vast majority of the houses are either detached or semi-detached. Traditionally it was home to wealthy Jewish businessmen but this has tended not to be the case since the 1980s. Lime Pictures, which used to be known as Mersey Television, is based in the area and is responsible for the production of Channel 4's *Hollyoaks*. Until their demise, Childwall was also where *Brookside* and *Grange Hill* were produced. Notable residents include or have included: Craig Charles (actor), Brian Epstein (businessman and manager of The Beatles in the 1960s), Ray Quinn (runner-up in *The X Factor* and all-round entertainer), Ian St John (footballer) and Edwina Currie (politician).

Garston

Distance from centre: 5.4 miles
Population: 17,000
Name origin: possibly from the Anglo-Saxon *gaerstun* 'grazing settlement' but there is some doubt about this.

Garston is an ancient settlement and certainly older than Liverpool itself. It is known to have been an outlying farm belonging to the ancient Saxon manor of West Derby and in medieval times there was a community of Benedictine monks there. Liverpool's expansion had a knock-on effect on Garston which also became more and more important because of its position almost at the widest point of the Mersey. It was an ideal place for shipping and docks and even today it is a thriving port for large container ships. Garston was not absorbed into Liverpool until 1902. Notable people born in Garston include: Les Dennis (TV personality), Billy Fury (pop idol of the 1950s and early '60s), Jack Jones (union leader), Rita Tushingham (actress) and John Aldridge, Paul Connolly and Steve Davies (all professional footballers).

Aigburth

Distance from centre: 4.7 miles
Population: 8,000 (approx.)
Name origin: a combination of Old Norse *eikr* 'oak tree' and
Anglo-Saxon *beorg* 'hill' so Aigburth is the 'hill where the oak
trees grow'.

The name is a pretty strong clue that this was one of the places
on the banks of the Mersey settled by the Norse or Viking
invaders who arrived in the tenth century. Today it is a prosperous
residential area known for its pleasant situation, greenery and
recreational amenities. Not least among them is Otterspool
Promenade, a strip of walk-way along part of the north bank of
the Mersey which is an ideal place for anyone who fancies a gentle
stroll or just wants to sit and watch the ships as they ply up and
down the river. It can be a pretty impressive sight, particularly
when a stately vessel is captured against the background of a
setting sun. Some past and present notable residents of Aigburth
include: Les Chadwick (guitarist with the 1960s pop group Gerry
and The Pacemakers), Gérard Houllier (football manager), Billy
Liddell (footballer), George Melly (jazz musician, author and art
critic), Ricky Tomlinson (actor) and Peter Calvocoressi (historian
and Second World War code-breaker).

Kirkdale

Distance from centre: 2.5 miles
Population: 16,000 (approx.)
Name origin: Anglo-Saxon *kirk* 'church' and *dele* 'dale', 'valley'
so Kirkdale was originally 'the church in the valley'.

Since Victorian times Kirkdale has been a predominantly
working-class area of Liverpool and it has had its fair share of
social and housing problems. Until the nineteenth century it
was a separate township and only became part of the expanding
Liverpool conurbation in about 1860. Much of the terraced
housing so typical of the area was built to accommodate the rapid
influx of labourers who settled there during Liverpool's period
of industrial growth. The poor living conditions in Kirkdale in
the nineteenth century gave rise to several fire-brand socialist

thinkers who considered it their role in life to right what they saw as social wrongs. Some past and present notable residents include Bessie Braddock (née Bamber, stalwart Labour politician), Victor Grayson and Jim Larkin (socialist activists), Brian Jacques (author) and April Ashley (the world's first person to have sex-change surgery).

Woolton
Distance from centre: 7 miles
Population: 15,000 (approx.)
Name origin: from the Anglo-Saxon *uluentun* 'Wulfa's farm'.

Woolton is another of the subsidiary farms belonging to the Saxon manor of West Derby. It was a separate village for most of its history and only became part of Liverpool in 1913. These days it is definitely a middle-class district and, despite changes over the years, has managed to retain much of the charm we associate with a bygone age. Its greatest claim to fame is probably its association with the birth of The Beatles; in 1957 John Lennon met Paul McCartney at a fête at St Peter's Church and they soon realised that they shared an interest in music. To borrow a well-worn cliché: the rest is history. Some notable residents, past and present, include John Lennon (musician) and it also seems a popular place with footballers: Fabio Aurélio, Dirk Kuyt, Pepe Reina, Fernando Torres, Ryan Babel and Steve Pienaar have all lived in Woolton.

Dingle
Distance from centre: 3 miles (approx.)
Population: 14,000 (approx.)
Name origin: *dingle*, a Middle English term for a deep or wooded hollow.

This is not the sylvan glade the name would suggest. It might have been when the land to the south of Liverpool was forest parkland where kings hunted deer. Now it a built-up area with lots of terraced houses in narrow streets leading down to the Cast-Iron shore (known locally as 'the Cazzy') which takes its name from the cast-iron foundry which used to be situated there.

Traditionally, Dingle was divided according to religious affiliation: the north tended to be Irish Catholic and the rest inhabited mainly by Welsh immigrants who were Protestant. Probably the most famous of the streets is Elswick Street where the 1980s television series *Bread* was set. Some notable former residents of the Dingle (locals tend to refer to the area as **the** Dingle) include Ringo Starr (Beatles drummer), Gerry Marsden (singer with Gerry and The Pacemakers), Billy Fury (singer) and the diminutive Arthur Askey (comedian).

West Derby
Distance from centre: 4.5 miles (approx.)
Population: 15,000 (approx.)
Name origin: Anglo Saxon *deor* 'wild animal' and Norse *by* 'village' so: 'the village where the wild animals roam'.

West Derby is much older than Liverpool and probably began life as a Saxon manor. We know that places such as Liverpool and Garston were outlying farms supporting the manor well before King John arrived on the scene. We also know that there was once a castle here but we cannot be sure of its exact position; the remains of what appears to have been a large wooden structure were discovered in the 1930s but whether or not they represent the site of the old castle is debatable. On the other hand, the old courthouse built in the time of Elizabeth I is still standing and there is evidence that the first court (the Wapentake court) was held in the village about 1,000 years ago. Today West Derby is a residential suburb of Liverpool and past residents have included Pete Best (original drummer with The Beatles), Bill Shankly (footballer and manager) and Carla Lane (writer). Sir Terry Leahy (Chairman of Tesco), Michael Edwards (actor) and Paul McGann (actor) were all educated in West Derby.

Wavertree
Distance from centre: 3 miles (approx.)
Population: 14,000 (approx.)
Name origin: possible from the Anglo-Saxon *waefer* 'waving' and *tre* 'tree', but not all linguists agree with this.

This is another of the ancient villages swallowed up by the ever-expanding urban sprawl of Liverpool. There is evidence of a Bronze Age settlement in the area, although the first mention of the place by name is *Wavretrue* in the Domesday Book. Of particular interest today to both historians and tourists is the 'roundhouse' which is in fact an octagonal lock-up, built in 1796, as a place of temporary restraint for miscreants and no doubt a place where many a drunk has been invited to sleep it off by the local constable. The district's other claim to fame is that it is home to Liverpool's only surviving grammar school, the Bluecoat School, which was founded in 1708. Notable residents past and present include George Harrison and John Lennon (Beatles) and Leonard Rossiter, Kenneth Cope, John Gregson and Norman Rossington (actors).

Everton

Distance from centre: 2.5 miles (approx.)
Population: 8,000 (approx.)
Name origin: from the Anglo-Saxon *eofor* 'wild boar' and *tun* 'enclosure' so the original place was famous for its boars.

Very close to the city centre, Everton was traditionally a rather run-down, working-class area of Liverpool. In the 1960s a slum-clearance scheme was initiated, much of the area was torn down and the people moved out to places such as the new estates in Kirkby. Scotland Road runs through Everton and always had a reputation for poverty and anti-social behaviour. Today nearly all the old houses (and the pubs!) have been demolished and much of the area resembles nothing more than an inner city motorway. Along with places such as Garston and Woolton, Everton was at one time a berewick of West Derby and until about 1780 was really just the small country parish of Walton-on-the-Hill (Walton's correct name). It was absorbed into Liverpool in 1835. One of Everton's main landmarks is Prince Rupert's Tower. Paradoxically, it hardly qualifies as a tower and it has nothing to do with Prince Rupert. It used to be thought that Prince Rupert hid in the building during the English Civil War, but as it was only built in 1787 this is obviously just local myth. It was in fact an eighteenth-century lock-up where drunks and petty criminals spent the night before

The incorrectly named Prince Rupert's Tower.

coming up before the magistrate in the morning. When it was in use it was referred to locally as Stewbum's Palace. This delightful epithet stems from the fact that, in those days, 'stewbum' was the colloquial term for people we would probably refer to as drunken layabouts.

RH&D LIGHT RAILWAY

When Liverpool redeveloped much of the derelict land around the docks area, one of the attractions the planners thought up for the Garden Festival was a narrow-gauge railway. This would have taken people all around the newly laid-out gardens and at the same time would have been a great experience for the kids. However, the money set aside simply would not allow the manufacture of the locomotives. So an engine and a few carriages were borrowed from the Romney, Hythe & Dymchurch Railway which daily conveys people to and fro over the Romney Marsh in Kent. Interestingly, the RH&DR was the brainchild of a certain rich landowner in Kent, Count Zborowski, who also happened to own the original car made famous in the film *Chitty Chitty Bang Bang*.

102 UPPER STANHOPE STREET

This rather unremarkable street not far from Liverpool's centre is linked to what has to be one of the most astonishing ironies of history. In 1911 a boy was born to a German living in the city and his Irish-born wife. He was Alois Hitler and his wife's maiden name was Brigit Dowling. Their new-born son was christened William Patrick Hitler. Alois was Adolf Hitler's half-brother and William Patrick was therefore the Führer's nephew. One of the very last bombs (some say the last) to fall on Liverpool during the May blitz of 1941 completely destroyed most of the houses in Upper Stanhope Street, including the one where the Hitlers had been resident.

JUMP SUNDAY

Everybody has heard of the Grand National, but only people of a certain age will remember Jump Sunday. Until about 1960 the Sunday before the Grand National horse race, the course was opened to the general public and they could walk around the course and take advantage of the stall-holders who set up shop for the day selling hot-dogs, ice-creams and making the whole event an enjoyable day out and creating a fairground atmosphere. But the most memorable character who never failed to put in an appearance was a tipster who went by the name of Prince Monolulu. He was a large black man, decked out in colourful clothes which included a brightly coloured cloak, a big red head-dress (complete with ostrich feathers) and who always carried an enormous umbrella. His catchphrase was 'I gotta horse, I gotta horse'. Unfortunately, he hardly ever predicted the winner, but nobody seemed to mind; he was appreciated more for his entertainment value than his skill at choosing winners.

And in fact the 'Prince' was just plain old Peter McKay who was born in the West Indies in 1881 and came to Britain in 1902 looking for work. He tried his hand at singing, playing the violin, lion-taming and fortune-telling before he hit on the idea of becoming a racing tipster. He died in 1965.

GONE BUT NOT FORGOTTEN – THE FLICS

From the 1930s to the 1960s nearly every part of Liverpool had its own cinema. But then television came along and the 'picture houses', 'pics' or 'flics' started closing down. Some became bingo halls, others were converted into supermarkets and others were simply flattened to make way for car parks or sites for high-rise flats. Here are some that are now little more than a footnote in Liverpool's social history:

Curzon	Old Swan
Casino	Prescot Road
Atlas	Rice Lane
Reo	Fazakerley
Majestic	London Road
Tatler	Church Street
Palace	Warbreck Moor
Carlton	Orrell Lane
Regent	Old Swan
Regal	Norris Green
Odeon	London Road
Rialto	Toxteth
Gaumont	Anfield
Futurist	Lime Street
Hippodrome	West Derby
Mayfair	Aigburth
Abbey	Wavertree
The Walton Vale	Walton Vale
Forum	Lime Street
Astoria	Walton Road
News Theatre	Clayton Square
Palais de Luxe	Lime Street
Scala	Lime Street
Bedford	Bedford Road
Carlton	Tuebrook

LIVERPOOL HUMOUR: EXAMPLE NINE

She's tuppence short of a full shillin'
She is not the most intelligent lady I have ever met

DID YOU KNOW?

The River Mersey is regarded as sacred by the Hindus living in Britain. They see it as a substitute Ganges.

Herman Melville, the American author, was so impressed by the size and scale of Liverpool's docks that he compared them to the Pyramids.

Several streets in the old part of Liverpool are called 'heys'. This is just an old word for 'field'.

Rafael Sabatini, the Italian-born author whose novel *Scaramouche* was turned into a Hollywood film in the 1950s starring Stewart Granger, spent part of his childhood in Maghull. His mother, Anna Trafford, was a Liverpool girl.

Bucking the trend somewhat, the cinema in Woolton with the rather unimaginative name 'The Picturehouse' reopened in 2007 after being closed down for several years.

4

LIVERPOOL'S GREAT AND GOOD

Liverpool does not only produce footballers, pop singers and soap stars. Starting with the ladies, here are many of the great and good of Liverpool who have made a considerable contribution to society and not just within the confines of their native or adopted city, but in the country as a whole:

CHERIE BLAIR

The wife of the former Prime Minister Tony Blair, Theresa Cara Booth, as she was christened, was born in 1954 in Bury, Lancashire, but brought up in Waterloo and Crosby. Her father is Tony Booth the actor who rose to prominence after taking a leading role in the 1960s TV sitcom *Till Death Us Do Part*. At school she showed an early aptitude for academic study which took her on to greater things. Her sharp mind and facility for acquiring facts led her to a First Class Honours degree at the London School of Economics and set her on course to a very successful legal career. She gained a pupillage in Derry Irvine's chambers where she met her future husband Tony Blair. Her progress within the legal profession followed a steady upward curve: in 1976 she became a barrister, then Queen's Counsel in 1995 and in 1999 was appointed Recorder (a sort of part-time judge) in County and Crown courts. But her career was not limited to the legal profession. She tried her hand at politics (although failed to get elected) and was awarded several academic honours and awards. From 1999 to 2006 she served as Chancellor of Liverpool John Moores University. She has also written her autobiography, a publication which brought her a certain amount of criticism for being perhaps a little too honest and open than some people felt was necessary. She provided personal (some might say intimate) details which many felt were too revealing and should have remained private. The book also contains the much-quoted episode of her husband's negotiations with Gordon Brown: when Tony was going to meet Gordon to discuss when he would hand over the reins to his colleague, Cherie apparently kissed him goodbye and told him not to bother coming home if Brown persuaded him to leave office after only one term.

Never content to remain in her husband's shadow, Mrs Blair has also set up the Cherie Blair Foundation, an organisation specifically designed to offer help and assistance on a worldwide basis to women entrepreneurs. The philosophy behind this foundation is quite simple: if we help the women who have the skills, drive and intelligence to set up and run their own businesses, the end result can only be beneficial. Successful businesses managed by enterprising women have a positive effect not only on their own families but on the whole communities in which they live and operate.

In addition to all this she has brought up four children and managed to find the time to acquire (together with her husband) a substantial portfolio of impressive properties in and around London.

BESSIE BRADDOCK

Elizabeth Bamber was born in Zante Street, Everton, in 1899. Her father was an easy-going man who took life as it came and took very little, if any, interest in the politics of the day. Her mother, on the other hand, was the archetypal socialist fire-brand who was determined that her daughter would grow up knowing the importance of fighting for human rights and social equality. And she made a pretty good job of it. As a young woman Bessie started to harangue her fellow man (and woman) about the need for Socialism in Britain, as she was painfully aware of the inequalities of life and opportunity in what was in fact a very rich country. But the rich were rich because they benefitted from the sweated labour of the majority. Some lived in easy luxury while others toiled from dawn till dusk, lived in rat-infested hovels and could barely afford enough to eat. And all the injustice of life in Britain during the first decades of the twentieth century was to be seen in microcosm in Liverpool; small wonder, then, that Bessie joined the Communist Party. And it was as a member of the CP that she met Jack Braddock, a man with political convictions as strong as hers. In 1922 they married and for the rest of their lives they struggled to improve the lot of the working men of Liverpool and bring some dignity to the lives of the thousands who endured an unbelievably harsh existence and reached the end of their lives with very little to show for it. In 1930 Bessie was elected MP for St Anne's Ward and then in 1945 was elected president of the Liverpool Trades Council. In the Second World War she served as a member of the ambulance service.

Bessie did not remain a member of the Communist Party for very long. She had joined because it seemed to offer the best way of winning workers' rights, but she became disillusioned with the failure of Communism to live up to its name and when reports filtered through of the party's excesses she turned against those whom she had formerly admired. But she still retained the fervour that won her the epithet 'Battling Bessie' and when she died her home town was a far better place to live in than when she was born. And much of the improvements were down to her.

She died in 1970 but she has not disappeared from Liverpool entirely. People arriving at Liverpool's Lime Street station are met by an effigy of Bessie, complete with handbag and briefcase, on the forecourt. It's a way of informing visitors, especially those who are visiting Liverpool for the first time, that the city they are about to become acquainted with was at the forefront in the battle for social equality in Britain.

EDWINA CURRIE

Another strong-minded lady, Edwina Currie (née Cohen) was as far away from Bessie Braddock in terms of position on the social scale as it is possible to be. She was born into a well-off Jewish family in 1946 in the Childwall area of Liverpool where her father was a successful businessman. Academically gifted she attended Liverpool Institute High School for Girls and then won a place at Oxford. She first intended to study chemistry but changed her mind and read Philosophy, Politics and Economics. On leaving Oxford she then moved to the London School of Economics where she gained her Master's degree in Economic History. It was while doing her research for this degree that she became convinced about the value of market forces and became a Conservative.

On graduating she took a job in Birmingham and then decided that she would try her hand at becoming a politician. She was elected in 1983 and represented South Derbyshire for 14 years. The Prime Minister of the day, Margaret Thatcher (who, coincidentally, also went up to Oxford to study chemistry), must have recognised a kindred spirit in Edwina as she appointed her to a position in the Department of Health. This turned out to be a double-edged sword: it could have been a considerable leg-up to high office but events conspired against her and caused a fall from grace from which the undoubtedly gifted, ambitious politician never recovered. In 1988 the country was faced with an outbreak of salmonella in chickens and the fear of food poisoning spread like wildfire. Sales of eggs fell and the producers began to feel the cold chill of an economic crisis. But then Edwina made the astonishing announcement that nearly all the eggs in the country were infected and the effect was immediate and catastrophic. There was very little evidence for her claim, but the damage was done. Egg production came to a virtual standstill; thousands of chickens were destroyed and the Farmers' Union was furious. Law suits flooded in, compensation had to be paid and Edwina had no option but to resign. She continued to represent her constituency until the General Election of 1997 but lost her seat and retired from politics. But she was only down; she was not beaten and she went on to carve herself a successful second career as a writer and a third as a broadcaster. Her energy and intellect, plus her tendency to express her strong opinions in a forthright manner led her erstwhile colleague Sir Julian Critchley to comment 'Edwina Currie has a brass neck, a silver tongue and a golden pen.'

KITTY WILKINSON

Out of the same mould as Bessie Braddock, Kitty had a heart of gold and, despite her own hard life, always seemed to reach deep down to find sympathy for her fellow man. She was born Catherine Seaward into an ordinary, working-class family in Londonderry (in what is now Northern Ireland) in 1786 where the struggle just to survive was harsh and never-ending. While Kitty was still a very small child her parents decided to leave Ireland to find a better life in England. But tragedy struck before they even landed. The ship on which they were passengers sank within sight of Liverpool and many drowned, including Kitty's father and sister. Kitty and her mother were rescued and somehow managed to eke out a living but exactly how it is impossible to say as we have no documents or evidence of any sort. All we do know is that when she was aged about twelve, Kitty went to work in a cotton mill in Lancashire where she learned just enough to keep body and soul together. At some point (probably in her late teens) she met and married a sailor and probably thought that her life now had at least a chance of improving, but she was seriously mistaken. After a couple of years of wedded bliss, relatively speaking, her husband was lost at sea and Kitty was left to bring up two very young children, at the same time as caring for her now aged and ailing mother.

When her mother died, Kitty thought she would have a better chance of finding some sort of work if she returned to Liverpool, which she did. She was horrified with what she found. Her own life was hardly one of unlimited luxury, but she found it difficult to come to terms with the conditions other people were living in. Anticipating Mrs Braddock a century later, Kitty decided she wanted to do something about the flea-ridden, rat-infested housing that many if not most of working-class Liverpudlians had to call home. At about the same time she met and married a warehouseman, Tom Wilkinson, a kind man who shared his new wife's concern for those even less fortunate than himself.

When one of the many cholera epidemics to visit the city broke out in 1832, Kitty rolled up her sleeves, as it were, and got to work trying to do something about it. It just happened that the Wilkinsons were the only people in the neighbourhood who had a hot water boiler in their kitchen and so Kitty invited everyone and anyone to bring their dirty linen for her to launder. They accepted her offer with alacrity and it then dawned on Kitty that what was needed in the area was some sort of facility where people could wash their clothes and bed linen. Of course the answer was a public wash-house. She immediately began pestering people of influence and, to cut a long story short, the first public wash-house in Liverpool was opened in 1842 in Upper Frederick Street. It was a small start in Liverpool's fight against filth and disease, but it was a start. Kitty died in 1860.

MIRABEL DOROTHY TOPHAM

An adopted daughter of Liverpool, Mirabel Topham (née Hillier) is arguably the main reason why people today can still enjoy a day out at the races in Liverpool. She was born in London in 1891, the daughter of a publican who happened to be the manager of the Theatre Royal, Haymarket, and so it was no real surprise to those around her when she went on the stage and then joined the line-up as one of the famous Gaiety Girls. She then married Ronald Topham, heir to a huge tract of land in Aintree which also just happened to be the home of the Grand National. In 1935 Mirabel took over the running of Aintree racecourse and did so very successfully for the next forty years. She had a very unhappy marriage and, psychologists might argue, devoted much of her energies into running the business as an escape from her sad home-life.

Mirabel was a formidable lady in every way. Her dancing girl figure did not last long. Her husband was fond of the good life and Mirabel was not one to let her husband's fondness for good food and wine lead him into a habit of solitary consumption. And pretty soon she was able to demonstrate an equally demanding fondness for a well-stocked pantry and wine cellar. Her willingness to entertain became legendary and she is reported as having said that ballooning up to 18 stones was a price she was willing to pay in exchange for the pleasure the lavish dinners gave her. But her life of luxury did not adversely affect her business acumen or her determination to have the racecourse run the way she wanted it run. Nobody argued with Mirabel: what Mirabel wanted, Mirabel got. Ronald took what was very much a back seat while his wife dreamed up more and more plans to make the course even more profitable. She designed and created a new race track, opened in 1953, within the existing one, naming it the Mildmay Course after Lord Mildmay, a skilled amateur jockey and passionate aficionado of the National. But the Queen Bee of Aintree (as she was nicknamed) was still not content: also in 1953 she opened a motor racing circuit which enjoyed considerable success until the 1960s as the venue for the European Grand Prix. In fact, this was the very circuit where the legendary racing driver Stirling Moss won his first grand prix in 1955. Jim Clark, another well-known competitor among the motor racing fraternity, won the same event in 1962. Mirabel died in 1980.

ANNE ROBINSON

Well-known, seemingly ubiquitous, TV personality and journalist Anne Robinson has carved out a career for herself by being unpleasant, if not downright obnoxious, to people who appear on her television show *The Weakest Link*. When the show first appeared on our screens in 2000 viewers were shocked by the way she attempted to humiliate her contestants and by the dismissive way she announced 'You are the weakest link – Goodbye!' It is not for nothing that she has earned the title 'The Queen of

Mean'. She describes herself as an unfit mother, and has made a public admission of her liking for more than just the odd drink. She also got herself into hot water for remarks she made on air about the Welsh, and was required to make a public apology for saying that she did not like them and did not know what they were for. She has also come in for some criticism over her support for fox-hunting and spoke out on several occasions against the fox-hunting ban introduced by Tony Blair's government. She has been quoted as saying she would lock up all those who support the ban because they just don't understand what it is that they are protesting against.

Anne Josephine Robinson was born in Crosby in 1944, the daughter of a schoolteacher father and entrepreneurial mother. She was fortunate enough to benefit from a private education at a school in Hampshire and enjoyed long holidays in the South of France with her parents. When the time came for her to decide on a career she chose journalism, a calling for which she has demonstrated more than her fair share of talent. Her first step up the ladder was to land a traineeship with the *Daily Mail* in 1967. From there she progressed to the *Sunday Times*, where she stayed for a number of years but for personal reasons was obliged to resign in 1978 and return home to Crosby. She then found a position with the *Liverpool Echo* where her journalistic experience and flair kept her in the north for a year or two. But by 1980 she was back in London, this time working for the *Daily Mirror*. Then, in 1982, her instinct led to a scoop which enhanced her reputation as a journalist but at the same time cost her her job. She was informed by somebody in the know that things were not as they should be between Prince Charles and Princess Diana. After some snooping around she was given a pretty strong hint from another reliable source that the princess was suffering from anorexia and the paper published the story. This did not make her any friends at the Palace and certain strings allegedly were pulled to have her removed. It was some time before the news of Diana's problems were officially admitted and Anne was vindicated, but by that time she had decided to develop her already burgeoning career in television.

Viewers now regularly saw Anne Robinson fronting the popular *Watchdog* consumer programme in which she and her team exposed dodgy workmen, rip-off merchants, cowboy builders and even energy companies who would not listen to customers' complaints over their bills. She has also made guest appearances in many other shows and is a frequent presenter on radio.

She has been divorced twice but is still very much on speaking terms with her former husbands. Her autobiography, which was published in 2001, has the disarmingly honest title *Memoirs of an Unfit Mother*. Anne Robinson is also a Fellow of Liverpool John Moores University.

LOTTIE DOD

Charlotte Dod was an amazing woman; in the annals of sporting history there can be few who have proved her equal in athletic prowess. She was one of those people who just seem to ooze sporting ability and excel at almost anything they set their minds to.

Lottie was born 'over the water' in Bebington in 1871, the daughter of Joseph and Margaret Dod. Her Liverpudlian father had gone into the rag trade and made a fortune dealing in cotton. In fact, his fortune was so great that neither Lottie nor her sister or two brothers ever had to do a day's work. The whole family was sports mad, but it was Lottie who went way beyond the bounds of what was thought achievable. She was born just two years before the invention of lawn tennis, and by the time she was in her early teens she was wielding a racquet with the best of them. If fact, she soon overtook everybody else and proved that she was the best. For some years she restricted her competitions to local events but by 1887 was confident enough, and capable enough, to get to Wimbledon and make it to the finals. To the amazement of just about everybody present, Lottie beat the defending champion Blanche Bingley 6–2, 6–0. After this, winning at Wimbledon became a bit of a habit and she went on to win no fewer than five times: 1887, 1888, 1891, 1892 and 1893.

For most people this would have been a remarkable achievement, but Lottie was not one to rest on her laurels. She had other sporting interests and in almost every one she achieved champion status. In 1897 she took up hockey and in next to no time was team captain. Her reputation, and that of her team, soon

spread and after leading her team to many victories, she eventually made it into the national team. In her first international match (March 1899) the team beat Ireland 3–1, and then in the rematch the following year England were again victorious, this time with a score of 2–1. And both goals were scored by Lottie.

After tennis and hockey, Lottie Dod also thought she would like to have a go at one or two other sports. Next on the list was golf and although ladies' golf had not yet been established, she was not one to be put off by such a minor detail. But now things were not quite so easy. In the first place golf clubs were very reluctant to admit ladies and so her opportunities for practice were somewhat restricted. In the second, she did not take to golf quite as readily as she had to other sports. She was not as successful as she had been on the tennis court and hockey pitch, but this does not mean that she was totally incompetent: she did play at international level, but her mantelpiece lacked the golfing trophies that might have kept the other trophies company.

Now it was the turn of the archers to see what Lottie Dod could do. She had been dabbling in the sport since the early years of the century and was soon up among the best in the country. She made it to the national championship finals, finishing fifth in 1906, 1907 and 1908. It was a remarkable achievement for one so inexperienced at the sport and was enough to win her a place in the British Olympic archery team. She ended up with the silver medal.

By now she was starting to lose interest a little in competitive sport. She had suffered for some years with sciatica and no doubt this forced her to cut down on her more physical activities. She never married and spent the latter part of her life in the south of England eventually dying, it is said, in a nursing home while listening to the radio coverage of Wimbledon in 1960. A more fitting exit for such a sporting lady would be very difficult to imagine.

GLENDA JACKSON

Here we have another example of a very talented lady from 'over the water'. Glenda Jackson was born in Birkenhead in 1936, the daughter of a bricklayer, and educated at the West Kirby County Grammar School for Girls. When she left school in about 1950 her first job was as a counter assistant in Boots but this was hardly likely to satisfy someone as talented as Glenda. Before very long she was on her way to London where she had gained a place at RADA. She had set her mind on becoming an actress and from the day she graduated she enjoyed a long and successful career both in theatre and in films, not to mention her unforgettable appearances on television. And there seemed to be no limit to her range: she could take on serious, dramatic roles such as her portrayal of Queen Elizabeth I, but she could also bring the house down with her slapstick performances with the comedy duo Morecambe and Wise. A measure of her ability can be judged from her successes: she began with *Separate Tables* (Terence Ratigan) in 1957 which was followed by a supporting role in the 1963 film *This Sporting Life*. In 1969 she played the starring role in *Women in Love* which brought her an Academy Award for Best Actress. After this the offers poured in and she made several TV appearances with Morecambe and Wise and starred in films such as *Sunday, Bloody Sunday* (1971), *The Boy Friend* (1971) and *Mary, Queen of Scots* (1971). In the same year she played the title role in *Elizabeth R*, a TV series for which she received a nomination for Best Actress (British Academy Television Award). For her services to the British film industry she was awarded a CBE in 1978.

But then it was all change. In the early 1990s Glenda Jackson decided that it was time for a career move and set her sights on politics. As a lady with strong left-of-centre convictions she supported the Labour Party and successfully stood as the candidate for Hampstead and Highgate in 1992. Five years later Tony Blair, who by now was Prime Minister and head of New Labour, appointed her junior minister with responsibility for London Transport. However, her relationship with New Labour and Tony Blair ceased to be amicable. She became more and more disillusioned with what was supposed to be a party of the Left as it seemed to behave more and more like the old Tory party it had replaced. Glenda became a vociferous backbencher who was never slow to criticise the leader of her party if she disagreed with him on a matter of principle. They never saw eye to eye on the matter of student top-up fees; he had decided to introduce them for all university students in England and she saw this as unacceptable. No less unpalatable for her was the Iraq War and when the Hutton Enquiry into the causes of the war and the strange circumstances surrounding the death of the government scientist David Kelly emerged, Glenda left no doubt in anyone's mind about her opinions. She even went so far as to demand the Prime Minister's resignation. In the 2010 election Glenda Jackson was re-elected with one of the smallest majorities in the country.

DID YOU KNOW?

Because of her involvement in the salmonella scare some of the press took to referring to Edwina Currie as 'Eggwina'.

When Anne Robinson left Liverpool to take up a job in London her mother gave her an MG sports car as a little gift to remind her of home.

Bessie Braddock was responsible for the adoption of the lion mark on British eggs as a sign of quality. Hence the statue of her on Lime Street station shows her holding an egg.

LIVERPOOL HUMOUR: EXAMPLE TEN

If yer can't see that, yer must need a bike on yer nose
If your vision is impaired you must need spectacles

ROBERT RUNCIE

Robert Alexander Kennedy Runcie (also titled The Right Reverend and The Right Honorable, The Lord Runcie), who eventually became Archbishop of Canterbury, was born in Crosby in 1921. There was nothing in his family background that might have hinted at the high office which he would eventually attain. By his own admission, the real reason he started attending church on a regular basis was the fact that he rather fancied a girl who went there as well. Nor was he encouraged in matters spiritual at home: his father (an electrical engineer at Tate & Lyle) leaned heavily towards atheism and is known to have professed a dislike of clergymen at the same time as a preference for horses of the racing variety. His mother was a hairdresser and of Irish descent. The family lived in Moor Lane, Crosby, and then moved to Queens Road, from where the young Robert attended Coronation Road Primary School. At the age of eleven he won a scholarship to one of Liverpool's most prestigious grammar schools, Merchant Taylors' and then, just before the outbreak of the Second World War, he won a place at Brasenose College, Oxford. But rather than take up his university place when the country was facing such a crisis, he joined the army and was given a commission in the Scots Guards. And it was as a serving officer (a tank commander) that Robert Runcie showed another side to his personality. The rather academic, somewhat introspective soldier demonstrated immense courage under enemy fire when he rescued the crew of a crippled tank and then, the very next day, drove his own tank straight at the enemy and knocked out three anti-tank positions. For these acts of conspicuous bravery he was awarded the Military Cross. At the end of the war he was among the first British troops to enter the Nazi concentration camp at Belsen where he was confronted with what was probably one of the most harrowing sights he had ever witnessed.

Back in England Robert Runcie returned to his unfinished business at Oxford, taking a First in Greats – Oxford University's term for Classics (Latin, Greek and Philosophy). He then moved to Cambridge to take a qualification in Theology before being ordained in the Diocese of Newcastle in 1950.

After some years in Newcastle he became Principal of Cuddesdon Theological College near Oxford and then in 1970 he was appointed Bishop of St Albans. Nine years later he was appointed to the 'top job' in the Church of England, becoming the Archbishop of Canterbury.

It is generally thought that Robert Runcie was a very successful archbishop, although his reign was not without problems and a certain amount of controversy. There were people in the Anglican Church who did not appreciate his willingness to accommodate the Pope and who made their feelings on the matter very clear. Nor did his willingness to ordain homosexual clergymen meet with a favourable response in every quarter and his refusal to oppose the ordination of women priests caused some traditionalists to feel that he had betrayed the Church. He died in 2000.

WILLIAM EWART GLADSTONE

William Gladstone who came to be known as the G.O.M. (Grand Old Man) of British politics was born at 62 Rodney Street, Liverpool, in 1809, a time when the area was still more rural than the built-up, decidedly urban part of the city it now is. His father was a Liverpool Scot who had acquired a considerable fortune in business and consequently young William's early years were spent in the cosseted surroundings of the privileged echelons of society.

He was educated first at a prep school in Seaforth and then went on to Eton and eventually Christ Church, Oxford, where he was an outstanding scholar. He graduated with a Double First in Classics and Mathematics. His love of Classics stayed with him for the rest of his life and his passion for the works of Homer seemed to increase as he got older. His success in mathematics, however, was a remarkable triumph as he possessed a self-confessed strong dislike of the subject.

When he graduated from university he followed the not uncommon route among the young well-to-do. He embarked on the Grand Tour of Europe visiting France, Belgium, Germany and Italy. Possibly it was on these travels that he contemplated taking up the law as a profession. Certainly, on his return to England, he enrolled as a law student with thoughts of becoming a barrister, but very soon changed his mind. At some point he realised that the law was not for him and that he would go into politics, and his contribution to Victorian England can hardly be over-estimated. He was Prime Minister four times (1868–74, 1880–5, Feb–July 1886 and 1892–4). He also served as Chancellor of the Exchequer four times (1852–5, 1859–66, 1873–4 and 1880–2).

William Gladstone is remembered now for his reforming zeal in some aspects of domestic and foreign policy, but when he first entered the House of Commons he was anything but a radical. In fact, he was quite reactionary. He opposed parliamentary reform, was against the abolition of slavery, saw no need to improve the lot of factory workers and was a firm believer that the State should support and defend the interests of the Church of England. But as time went on Gladstone became far more democratic in his outlook and in 1859 joined the Liberals, supporting their moves for reform of the legal system and an overhaul of the powers and practices of the Civil Service. He was a firm supporter of the movement to grant home rule to Ireland and advocated support for the Balkan nations who were suffering cruel oppression at the hands of the Turks in what was then the Ottoman Empire.

In 1839 Gladstone married Catherine Glynne with whom he enjoyed a happy 59-year marriage, a union which bore the couple no fewer than eight children. The Glynne family owned the Hawarden Estate in Flintshire, North Wales, and William and his wife lived there for the rest of their lives. The estate has survived to this day and is still the home of William and Catherine's descendents. It also houses the enormous personal library which William accrued over his long, active and eventful life. William died in 1898.

SIR JOHN MOORES

Although not a native Scouser, John Moores has to count as one of Liverpool's most illustrious adopted sons. He was born into a family of very limited means in 1896 in Eccles, Lancashire, and was one of eight children. Their father was a bricklayer who seems to have spent less and less time laying bricks and more and more time knocking back pints of beer. When he died at the young age of 47 (officially of tuberculosis, but his fondness for the bottle would not have helped) the family found it hard to cope.

John, meanwhile, had been demonstrating a desire and determination to improve his lot. Although he was forced to leave school at the age of fourteen, he decided that he wanted a better life than the one his parents had been forced to endure. His first job was with the Manchester Post Office as a messenger boy but within a very short time found himself a student at the Post Office School of Telegraphy. In 1912 he moved to the Commercial Cable Company where his background in telegraphy secured him a steady job, but by 1916 he had joined the Navy as a wireless officer and telegraphist. He was demobbed after the war, in March 1919, and went back to his old employers who posted him to Liverpool, where, after another brief posting to Ireland, he spent the rest of his life.

Moores was an avid follower of football, both as a spectator and player, and of course he was not alone. He had two long-standing friends in Bill Hughes and Colin Askham who shared his passion and the three of them put their heads together to see if they could combine their sporting interests with some way of making money. It was about this time also that Moores heard of a system devised by one John Jervis Bernard which would harness people's dreams of earning significant amounts of money, by having a flutter now and again, and his interest in football. Bernard had hit on the idea of a football 'pool' which involved getting people to subscribe to a 'pool' of money and then attempting to forecast a certain number of match results. The winner or winners would be paid out of the pool, but a percentage would obviously be held back to cover costs and the salaries of the people operating the scheme. It sounded a good idea, but Bernard could not make it pay and so Moores, Hughes and Askham took it over, forming a company in 1923 which they named the Littlewood Football Pool (Askham had been born Colin Henry Littlewood but was orphaned at an early age and took the surname of the aunt who adopted him, though it was decided to 'borrow' his birth name). But the scheme still never took off and Hughes and Askham withdrew. They were convinced that they had given it their best shot and that putting any more money into the business would be sending good money after bad. But Moores was made of sterner stuff; he was sure that it was just a question of time and a little more determination. And how right he was. He was not an overnight success, but he kept slogging away at the business and eventually it began making a profit. By 1932 John Moores was a millionaire. But he was still a young man and was not the type to just sit back and enjoy a life of luxury. He began looking around for a new challenge and came up with the idea for a new concept in the art of selling and practice of buying; the new concept would allow people to choose goods from a catalogue, order them by post and have them delivered a week or so later. In no time at all he had the whole thing up and running as the Littlewoods Mail Order Store. In 1937 he then opened the first of many retail stores.

John Moores married Ruby Knowles in 1923 and they had a long and happy marriage which resulted in the birth of four children. They bought a house in Formby in 1930 and remained there for the rest of their lives. Ruby died in 1965 and John chose not to leave the house which held so many happy memories for him. He was knighted in 1980 and when he died in 1993 he left a fortune estimated at some £10 million. The John Moores University Liverpool is so named in his honour.

JEREMIAH HORROCKS

When he died on 3 January 1641 Jeremiah Horrocks had achieved more to write himself into the history books than most people manage in the full span of three score years and ten. He had taken on the best scientists of the time and shown that the great minds such as those possessed by Johannes Kepler and Tycho Brahe, the pioneers in the field of astronomy, were no match for a boy from Toxteth. The young Jeremiah was fascinated by the physical world about him to such an extent that he became a passionate student of mathematics and mechanics and then turned his not inconsiderable intellect to the study of astronomy, a subject which was about to guarantee his immortality.

He was born in the Toxteth Park area of Liverpool in 1618 where his father was a farmer and so hardly able to afford to gather together the funds to provide an expensive education for his son. Jeremiah, however, did sufficiently well (presumably by his own effort and determination) to became a student at Cambridge as a 'sizar'. This meant that he was permitted to attend lectures and receive tuition free of charge in return for performing certain duties and menial tasks within his college.

Whether or not Jeremiah Horrocks ever finished his degree is open to some discussion. Some sources say that he graduated, others say that, even as a sizar, the costs of being a student were just too great and that he left without a formal qualification.

What is not in doubt, however, is his increasing interest in all things connected with astronomy. He studied the texts available at the time and familiarised himself with the works of the German astronomer Kepler (1571–1630) and the Dane Tycho Brahe (1546–1601), and began to question their findings and assertions. At the tender age of seventeen he was already hinting that astronomers should consider following different lines of enquiry and is credited with being the first person to show that the moon follows an elliptical track around the earth. It is also claimed that he became interested in the phenomenon of unseen forces and embarked on a mathematical examination on the force we now take for granted and recognise as gravity. If he really did make a start on research of this nature he anticipated the work later done by Isaac Newton.

But the calculation for which Jeremiah Horrocks will always be remembered concerned the transit of Venus across the surface of the sun. He was living in the village of Much Hoole, near Preston, at the time where he was curate in the local church. He calculated that Venus would follow a course across the surface of the moon and would be visible from earth at 3.00 p.m on 24 November 1639 (Julian calendar) or 4 December (Gregorian calendar). His prediction was at variance with Kepler's calculations and, as 3 o'clock ticked by and there was no sign of Venus, it began to look as though Horrocks was wrong and Kepler right. But then, at 3.15 p.m., a black dot could be detected moving from one side of the sun to the other. Horrocks had been proven right. It was a remarkable achievement for one so young whose only equipment was, by our standards, primitive in the extreme.

When he suddenly died in his early twenties it was shock to all concerned. Liverpool, England and the worldwide scientific community had been unceremoniously robbed of one of history's most brilliant minds.

BRIAN EPSTEIN

Known, at least unofficially, as the Fifth Beatle, Brian Epstein was of Russian and Lithuanian descent. His grandparents had arrived from Eastern Europe in about 1900 and set up a business in Walton Road. It was supposed to be a furniture business but it also sold musical instruments and, as fate would have it, it was this side-line that was to determine young Brian's fate, not to mention that of a certain group of four young Liverpool musicians.

Born in 1934, originally Brian Epstein was destined for a career in the retail industry, although it has to be said that such a fate was his father's idea, not his. He had artistic inclinations and even expressed a wish to become an actor or dress designer, but his father was not too keen on the idea. When the family business began to expand, one of its first moves was to take over NEMS (North End Music Store) in Great Charlotte Street, offering clients the chance of buying guitars, pianos, etc. on very favourable 'never-never' terms. Epstein *père* put Brian in charge of the first floor and then, when the family empire expanded even further, Brian was put in charge of the whole new store which opened on Whitechapel.

It was a demanding job, but Brian still found time to indulge his interest in more artistic pursuits, including music. And as fate would have it, the new store was less than the proverbial stone's throw from the dirty former warehouse which had been taken over by musicians of all sorts and which the world would come to know as The Cavern. On a visit to The Cavern to hear a lunch-time session, Brian was star-struck. He watched a scruffy foursome as they caterwauled their way through a song and belted out the tune on drums and guitars. Not everybody in the audience was impressed, but Brian was. He was struck by their stage presence, their sense of humour and general aura of success lurking beneath an unappealing outer persona. Within weeks he found himself offering them a five-year contract and we all know the rest. Now he began a programme of transformation: he told them to smarten up (it was still the pre-grunge age), wear well-cut suits, have a hair-cut and to bow in unison at the end of every performance. This was 1961 and the next few years saw The Beatles, skilfully managed by the ex-furniture shop manager, go from strength to strength, but they were not the only ones. Brian had found his niche and soon other performers such as Gerry and The Pacemakers, Cilla Black and Billy J. Kramer were under his wing and heading for stardom.

Brian's death was a shock. He was apparently in good health and most people thought that he was just at the beginning of what was to be a magnificently successful career. When the news broke on 27 August 1967 that he had died in his London house at the age of thirty-two, it was not only his nearest and dearest who were stunned; the whole world was. Officially the cause of death was an accidental drug overdose, but rumours circulated that it might have been suicide. We probably will never know the real truth, but what is certain is that while he was alive, Brian Epstein's contribution to the world of popular music was inestimable and the service he performed for his native city incalculable.

JOHN BIRT, BARON BIRT

Not exactly a 'rags-to-riches' story but the saga of the rise and rise of John Birt almost falls into that category. He was born in Liverpool (to be precise, Walton Hospital) in December 1944 where his father worked for the Prudential Insurance Company, earning just about enough to cover the mortgage. The family was not destitute, but there was little or no cash for anything but the bare essentials. His father was a devout Catholic and the young John was given a decidedly Catholic education at St Mary's College in Crosby, a school run by the Christian Brothers and renowned for its strict discipline. He then gained a place at St Catherine's College, Oxford, to study engineering. This was a considerable achievement but not one crowned with glittering success as, at the end of his three-year course, he was only awarded a third-class degree.

However, he would make up for his lack of degree certificates to hang on his study wall later – for his contributions to broadcasting he was awarded a string of honorary doctorates by several universities, including Liverpool John Moores University and the City University in London. And of course there is his progress up the social ladder from relatively humble beginnings in a Liverpool semi to Peer of the Realm.

He is known by those who know him as a somewhat reserved, almost reticent man but at the same time a man who has an iron will and a determination to see his plans through to fruition, whatever the cost. Possibly, this quiet confidence and inner strength explains why, at the tender age of seventeen, he was sure enough of himself to take on the part-time job as a bouncer at the Cambridge Hall, Southport, to earn a bit of extra cash. By coincidence, one of his first stints on the door was at a concert in which an up-and-coming group from Liverpool who called themselves The Beatles was playing.

When he left Oxford his engineering degree was probably not good enough to secure him a career in engineering and so he applied to be taken on as a graduate trainee at the BBC. He was not offered a place, but then managed to get taken on as a production trainee by the independent TV company Granada, based in Manchester. He had only been in the job for less than a year when he scored a major scoop; he persuaded Mick Jagger of the Rolling Stones to be interviewed by William Rees-Mogg. Jagger had recently spent a few days in gaol for smoking cannabis and the interview was intended as a dialogue between the generations. From then on it was upwards all the way. He climbed the promotion ladder at a fairly steady pace over the next couple of decades, at times with independent television and at others with the BBC. Eventually, in 1992, he was appointed Director General of the BBC and remained in post until 2000.

During his time as the DG, he oversaw the early stages of major revolutions in broadcasting. Digitalisation and interactive TV, not to mention satellite and cable TV, meant that a steady helmsman was need to steer the corporation between the rocks and whirlpools in the ocean of emerging media innovations. There are conflicting opinions as to how successful Birt was as Director General, and he certainly did not always see eye-to-eye with those who worked with him. He had a particular dislike for what he saw as the dumbing-down of the media. His famous remarks about the 'tabloidisation' of television and its increasing reliance on programmes which are made with the sole intention of humiliating members of the public won him few friends among other media executives.

When he was knighted and then, in 1999, given a Life Peerage, John Birt came in for some vitriolic criticism from the unions. When they heard of his award, and the fact that he had increased his own already substantial salary, they were aghast. This was the man who had sacked hundreds of employees and was now, as they saw it, enjoying the fruits of his own willingness to wield the axe.

JAMES LARKIN JONES

Born in a working class family in Garston in 1913, Jack Jones (as he was known) spent his life fighting for better conditions for dockers, the working man, pensioners and just about anybody who, in his opinion, deserved better treatment from the society in which he lived. Like Bessie Braddock, Jack became a member of the Communist Party, but unlike Bessie, he did not have a change of heart about Communism and remained a Party member for just about all of his adult life.

When he left school at the age of fourteen he was taken on as an apprentice electrical engineer and probably looked forward to a lifetime of steady employment and security, if not an enormous salary. But then came the Wall Street Crash and Jack Jones's world, like that of many workers, fell apart. His job disappeared and just about the only employment he could find was as a Liverpool docker. It was also at about this time that he read a novel which was to have a profound on his life and thinking. The novel in question was *The Ragged Trousered Philanthropists* by Robert Tressel, an uncompromising analysis of the ills of capitalist society. It was based on Tressel's personal experiences and told of his own awakening to socialist philosophy. Its harrowing description of the plight of the ordinary man who wants nothing more than to be allowed to earn enough money to support a wife and family with a certain amount of dignity and in reasonable comfort, struck a note with Jones.

But Jack was no mere theorist. His burgeoning socialist ideas and ideals were put to the test in the 1930s when Fascism began to raise its ugly head. Jones took part in street fights against Moseley's 'Black Shirts' and, when the civil war broke out in Spain, was among the first to enlist to fight on the side of the International Brigade against Franco's Fascists. At the Battle of Ebro in Catalonia in 1938 Jack Jones was seriously wounded. This was one of the longest and most bloody battles of the whole war, and in fact was the battle that put the final nail in Republicanism's coffin. Jack had taken part in the battle that marked the end of the Republican army as an effective fighting force.

Back home to recover from his wounds, Jack did not accept that the war against Fascism was over, but he was no longer fit enough to don a uniform. His fight, as he saw it, could continue in the workplace as he struggled to win better wages and conditions for the working man. He became a full-time official with the TGWU (Transport and General Workers' Union) in Coventry and, while fighting for what he termed 'workers' democracy' he also became involved with politics as an active and very forceful member of the

Labour Party. In the 1970s, when union power was an ever-present challenge to elected governments, Jack Jones was considered to wield more power even than the Prime Minister.

But there is, allegedly, another side to Jack Jones' career. In some quarters he is suspected of having let his intense dislike of Fascism go too far. He never hid the fact that he was member of the Communist Party and there have been allegations that he cosied up to Moscow a little too closely during the days of the old Soviet Union. Oleg Gordievsky, the high-ranking KGB officer who defected to the west before the fall of the Communism, claims that Jones passed information to the Russians for over forty years. Jack always denied this, and indeed threatened to sue anyone who alluded to the accusations, but the academic historian and security expert Christopher Andrew repeated Gordievsky's assertions in his history of MI5, *The Defence of the Realm*, and we can only assume that he would not have done had he not been reasonably sure of his facts. Jack Jones died in 2009.

LIVERPOOL HUMOUR: EXAMPLE ELEVEN

''Er old fellah's egg-shell blond'
Her husband is bald

DID YOU KNOW?

The playwright Dennis Potter referred to John Birt as a 'croak-voiced Dalek'.

John Moores persuaded the legendary footballer Dixie Dean to play in his baseball team.

Sir Paul McCartney's family bought a piano from Epstein's furniture store long before The Beatles hit the pop scene.

Jack Jones was nicknamed 'the Emperor' by union bosses.

LIVERPOOL HUMOUR: EXAMPLE TWELVE

'If yer wuz in Venice you could 'ire them out for gondolas'
The shoes you are wearing appear to be rather large to me

5

LIVERPOOL'S MAGNIFICENT ARCHITECTURE

Until a generation or so ago Liverpool was mainly known for its slums. With the possible exception of the Three Graces and St George's Hall, much of the city's architectural heritage was largely unknown to those who had never set foot in the city or bothered to read about the beautiful buildings the city had to offer. Few people, for instance, even today realise that there are more listed buildings in Liverpool (2,500) than in any other city in the country outside London. So let's have a look at the main ones.

THE PARISH CHURCH

The Parish Church, or the Church of Our Lady & St Nicholas, separated from the water's edge by the roads skirting the Pier Head, stands on or very near to the site of one of the original buildings that made up the embryonic hamlet of Liverpool in the thirteenth century. The original chapel which graced the coastline in the thirteenth century was the Chapel of St Mary del Key (or Quay), founded shortly after King John granted Liverpool its charter in 1207. Later on, between 1355 and 1361 a new chapel was built, this time dedicated to St Mary and St Nicholas and in 1515 the Crosse family (one of Liverpool's oldest) established a grammar school in the church thus marking the beginnings of an educational system in the borough.

In February 1810 disaster struck. The building had been left to fall into a state of disrepair and, although the parishioners knew the masonry needed attention, they never actually got round to

The grounds of St Nicholas's Church.

doing anything about it. Then, as the church was filling up for Sunday service, the bells, as they were calling the faithful to their devotions, collapsed and crashed through the roof. Twenty-five souls were killed and about the same number injured. Repairs were carried out and then, over the years, bits were added here and there until a new church had been built.

The next time disaster struck, the cause had nothing to do with the parishioners. This time it was Herr Hitler and his bombers who were to blame: in 1940 the church was virtually destroyed during an air-raid, and work on reconstruction only began in 1949. The new building was consecrated in 1952.

Some facts
In 1746 when the spire was added to St Nicholas's Church, its purpose was not theological. It had a far more practical use: it was to act as a navigational aid for ships approaching the port.

In 1695 pews were constructed for the sole use of the choir and this is thought to be the first time a choir was given its own set of pews in an English church.

ST JOHN'S BEACON
(AKA 'RADIO CITY TOWER')

This was, until recently, the tallest building in Liverpool and it towered, quite literally, over everything in the vicinity. The architects who designed it in 1969, Weightman and Bullen, originally intended it as a part of the ventilation system for St John's Market at the tower's base, but it was never used for that purpose. Instead it became a bit of a novelty: an enormous tower poking into the sky with a revolving restaurant at the top. In the 1970s diners could enjoy a meal (barring low cloud) and watch the environment gradually change as the restaurant turned on its own axis. But by 1977 fears for its safety had arisen and so the Liverpudlians who fancied a meal out had to find a more earthly venue for their epicurean delight. There was an attempt to reopen the restaurant in the 1980s but it turned out to be a business flop; people seemed to have lost their appetite for revolving dinners! In about 2000 the building underwent another transformation and, after a £5,000,000 refurbishment, it became a radio station and continues as such today.

St John's Beacon.

Some facts

There are 558 stairs leading to the top of St John's Beacon.

It also has two lifts which travel from ground level to the top in 30 seconds.

When it reopened in 1983 the restaurant had a 'Buck Rogers' space theme.

THE WEST TOWER

The crown for the tallest building in Liverpool has now been transferred to the magnificent head of the West Tower, which stands like a lofty aristocrat of the Pier Head, refusing to stoop to the baser crowd. It was built between 2005 and 2007 by Carillion (the architects were Aedas) at a cost of £35,000,000. At 459ft it dwarfs everything for miles around to such an extent that diners in the sky-high restaurant can look *down* on the old iconic buildings such as the Parish Church and even the Liver Buildings with its two famous birds! On a clear day it offers views over the Wirral in one direction and even as far as Blackpool, 30 miles up the Lancashire coast, in the other. The forty-storey-high skyscraper has what is known in architectural circles as an 'animated façade'. In other words, the exterior is fully glazed and comprises randomly selected opaque and clear sheets of glass which are affected by light and temperature in such a way as to create the impression of constant movement.

Some facts

The West Tower is also known as the Beetham Tower West, although the locals also refer to it as 'The Bullet'.

It ain't cheap! Anyone who wants to rent one of its 2-bedroom apartments will have to fork out up to £900 per calendar month and, for a penthouse, up to £2,500 (2011 rates).

ORIEL CHAMBERS

Perhaps not one of the first buildings that springs to mind when considering the architecture of Liverpool given that it is hidden away, modestly standing among its brasher counterparts in the banking and legal quarter of the city. Nevertheless, Oriel Chambers, designed by Peter Ellis and built in 1864, marked a new phase in the development of Liverpool buildings and a serious attempt to deal with the problem of interior lighting. Situated on Water Street the façade in some ways anticipates the West Tower as it reduces the brickwork to a minimum and makes maximum use of glass. At the time, it was not particularly well received as it abandoned many of the traditional approaches to building construction. Some critics even described it as little more than a greenhouse that had gone mad. However, its place in history can be assured as it is the very first example of curtain-wall construction and later became the blueprint for the skyscrapers of New York.

THE ROYAL LIVER BUILDING

The most famous building on the Liverpool skyline is, without a doubt, the Royal Liver Building. Together with the Cunard Building and the Port of Liverpool Building it is one of the Three Graces and probably the most famous port building in the world. Generations of sailors have felt their hearts skip a beat when, after months at sea, they got the first glimpse of the Liver Building as their ships entered the mouth of the Mersey. With its famous birds it has become a symbol of home for travellers and Scouser ex-pats, no matter how long they have been away.

The architect of this iconic building was Birkenhead-born Walter Aubrey Thomas (1859–1934) and building work began in 1908. By 1911 all thirteen storeys were complete and the new offices for the Royal Liver Assurance Company were open for business. Standing at an impressive 295ft it was once the tallest building in the city but has now been superseded by, firstly, St John's Beacon and then West Tower.

Some facts

One of the clock faces, all of which are 25ft in diameter, was used as a dining table by the directors of the Royal Liver Society before it was lifted into position.

The Royal Liver Building is a Grade I listed building.

The Royal Liver Building has a total of 16 lift shafts although only 12 have been in operational use since the 1970s.

One local joke about the birds says that one is watching the shipping and the other watching the football.

According to another the bird facing the city is male and is watching to see if the pubs are open while the other, female, is looking out to see if any handsome matelots are sailing up the Mersey.

Yet another says that if a virgin walks across the Pier Head the birds flap their wings. The birds' wings have never been known to move.

The building is protected with a reinforced concrete shell made of 25,000 tonnes of Norwegian granite.

THE CUNARD BUILDING

The second of the Three Graces, the Cunard Building, is very different from the Liver Building. The Liver Building reaches to great heights and might be said to symbolise Liverpool's aspirations to tower above the country's other ports in importance and achievement. The Cunard Building, on the other hand, is solid, squat and less ornate, reflecting the serious business of its original inhabitants: caring for the passengers who sailed to and fro across the Atlantic on voyages which were not entirely without risk. On the outside the building is a mixture of Italian Renaissance and Greek revival style, but the inner shell is reinforced concrete, as is that of the building's close neighbour, the Royal Liver.

The architects for the Cunard Building were William Edward Willink (1856–1924), another Birkenhead boy, and Philip Coldwell Thicknesse (1860–1920) and they began work on the building in 1914, completing it in 1917. During the Second World War the basement of the building was strengthened and altered so that it could double as an air-raid shelter, not only for the people employed in its myriad of offices, but for employees from the surrounding businesses. The vaults in the basement are particularly strong and even today serve as the repository for many valuable historical artefacts and documents relating to the history of shipping in Liverpool.

THE PORT OF LIVERPOOL BUILDING

The third of the Graces, although in fact the first one to be built (it was completed in 1907), is the Port of Liverpool Building (formerly the Mersey Docks and Harbour Board). A visitor to the city seeing this edifice for the first time could be forgiven for mistaking it for a church. The domed roof (soaring 220ft into the air) makes the whole thing resemble St Peter's Basilica in Rome or St Paul's Cathedral in London, but there is absolutely nothing spiritual about this building. The similarity to a baroque style church is sustained on the interior, but the ornamentation is not directed at the theologically impressionable. When the edifice was built its sole purpose was to provide offices for those employed in the day-to-day running of the port. The perhaps excessive grandeur of the interior is simply an indication of how the architects' imaginations were allowed to run wild. The architects involved were Sir Arnold Thornley, F.B. Hobbs and the firm Briggs and Wolstenholme.

Although the Royal Liver Building is probably now the most famous of the Three Graces, architects generally consider the Port of Liverpool Building to be the jewel in the crown of Liverpool's Pier Head. Incidentally, the architect Sir Arnold Thornley also designed Stormont, the parliament buildings in Belfast, Northern Ireland.

THE TOWN HALL

No less imposing in its architectural majesty is the Town Hall. It is a match for any of the newer buildings at the Pier Head but has a much longer history than all, apart from the Parish Church. The first Town Hall, which was really nothing but a thatched barn, was donated to the emerging mercantile city by the Reverend John Crosse, the same man who had opened the town's grammar school near the water's edge. The second, more substantial building was opened in 1673 on the orders of the then mayor, James Jerome. This building was referred to mainly as the Exchange for the simple reason that local merchants and businessmen would gather there to discuss matters of business and to 'exchange' deals, contracts and the other paraphernalia of commerce. Less than 100 years later it was decided that an even more impressive building was needed to reflect the success of the entrepreneurs who had made it their spiritual home. A certain John Wood of Bath was approached in 1748 and asked to take charge of a new, more imposing building to grace Liverpool's business quarter. He agreed, set to work and in 1754 a magnificent new building provided pleasant surroundings in which the great and the good of Liverpool's business community could meet and seal their deals. Unfortunately, many of the 'great and the good' were not so good and owed much of their greatness to their involvement in the slave trade. In fact, it is thought that no fewer than sixteen of Liverpool's former mayors grew fat on the money they earned from what was euphemistically called the 'African trade'.

In 1795 Wood's building was almost completely destroyed by fire. Work on the restoration began almost immediately under the direction and guidance of the London architect James Wyatt. However, Wyatt was a bit of a perfectionist who refused to be rushed and it took him fifteen years to complete the job. That said, the end product was a beautiful building, not that much different from the one which evokes such admiration today. Sadly, however, this building too had its share of misfortune. In the May blitz of 1941 the building was seriously damaged by a German bomb and so, once again, had to go through a prolonged process of reconstruction and repair. But this time the building that emerged was the beautiful example of neoclassical architecture that looks majestically down Castle Street today.

Some facts

In 1881 Irish rebels tried to blow the building up but the device was spotted and dragged away by the local bobby.

Rioting sailors in the eighteenth century used their ship's cannon to fire on the Town Hall. Fortunately, according to accounts of the day, they were too drunk to aim straight and so little if any damage was done.

The dining room contains two huge ornamental vases but nobody has ever been able to identify their place of origin. It is believed that they are from somewhere in the Far East, but beyond that, nobody can be absolutely sure.

In 1818 gas lighting made its appearance in Liverpool and the very first building to have it installed was the Town Hall.

ST GEORGE'S HALL

If all this were not enough, for sheer magnificence on an enormous scale there can be few sights anywhere in Britain to rival the stately grandeur of the city's architectural centrepiece: St George's Hall. Standing on the site of what used to be the Liverpool infirmary ((1749–1824) this colossus of neoclassical architecture (a Grade I listed building) looks as if it had been lifted by some Titan and transposed from ancient Athens to the banks of the Mersey.

When the idea was first mooted to build a grand edifice on what was then the edge of the city, the planners' idea was to build a venue for the musical events which were proving so popular among the wealthier classes of Liverpool. It was also decided that a competition should be held to choose the architect and it was won by Harvey Lonsdale Elmes. Work began in 1841 and was completed in 1854. Unfortunately, Elmes did not see his creation in its finished form; he went abroad for health reasons only to be stricken by some nasty infection and promptly died. The work had to be completed by Sir Charles Cockerell.

The exterior of the building is adorned with a combination of Corinthian columns and square, unfluted pillars interspersed with nereids and tritons (in Greek mythology the nereids were sea nymphs and the tritons mermen and messengers of the gods beneath the waves). The interior is no less ornate, with law courts and concert halls at opposing ends. The main concert hall measures an enormous 169ft by 77ft by 82ft and the highly ornate floor is made of Minton tiles. The various niches which surround the floor contain statues of local and national dignitaries such as William Roscoe, Robert Peel, George Stephenson and William Ewart Gladstone.

Some facts
Children who grew up in Liverpool before the early 1960s thought that St George's Hall was built of black stone. It was only when the building was cleaned of all the soot and grime that had discoloured it over the years that people realised what the original colour was.

The floor of the central concert hall is made up of over 30, 000 tiles.

An interior bronze door bears the letters SPQL standing for the Latin *Senatus Populusque Liverpudliensis* i.e. 'The senate and people of Liverpool'.

In 2007 and 2008 the concert hall was converted into a huge indoor skating rink.

There are other St George's Halls in Bradford, Bristol, Blackburn and Reading.

THE WALKER ART GALLERY

During the nineteenth century there were two sides to Liverpool. There were the dreadful slums where people endured a degree of poverty we find it hard to imagine today, but at the same time there was an awakening cultural awareness among the better-off. St George's Hall, as we have seen, was originally built as a venue for musical events for the delectation of Liverpool's increasingly enlightened bourgeoisie. Just over the road, however, other aspects of the arts were soon to be catered for. Andrew Walker, a former mayor and wealthy industrialist, donated a huge sum of money to the town in 1877 for the construction of the Walker Art Gallery which continues even today to delight visitors from far and wide with the excellence of its collection of paintings and sculptures. During the Second World War it was severely damaged by incendiary bombs but fortunately, enough of the original façade survived for the building to be restored to its former glorious self in the 1960s. In the same block is the Picton Library, a reference and lending library designed by Sir James Picton and opened in 1879, and one of Liverpool's Museums. All in all, the whole block is a magnificent neoclassical adjunct to St George's Hall so that this part of Liverpool offers a cityscape that is second to none in Europe, if not the whole world. And just to finish it off, all these buildings overlook St John's Gardens, a haven of peace and tranquillity in the midst of a very busy city.

LIVERPOOL CATHEDRAL

Most of the buildings we have looked at so far have been commercial, but there are buildings in Liverpool which cater for the more spiritual side of human existence. There are the two cathedrals, very different from each other architecturally, and places of worship which cater for Liverpool's adherents of other faiths: three mosques and four synagogues.

The Anglican cathedral is yet another outstanding example of English architecture and no less a figure than Sir John Betjeman referred to it as one of the most beautiful buildings in the world. It towers over the centre of the city and the River Mersey from its vantage point on St James's Mount like a giant, red sandstone (quarried in Woolton) sentinel.

Curiously, the Anglican cathedral was a bit of an afterthought. When the diocese was created in 1880 Liverpool had no cathedral and the old St Peter's Church, which used to stand roughly where Topshop/Topman is now on Church Street, was used as a 'pro-cathedral'. Then, in 1902, after much discussion, the city fathers decided that there was no point having a diocese without a cathedral and plans went ahead to organise a competition for the best design. A very young Giles Gilbert Scott produced a design which pleased the judges and he was awarded the contract. In

The Anglican cathedral.

1904 King Edward VII laid the foundation stone and work began. But it was a very slow process. Not only did the architect change his original designs considerably, but financial constraints and two world wars slowed down the construction work to a huge extent. It was not until 1940 that regular services began and the central tower, probably the cathedral's distinguishing feature, was not completed until 1942. The final moment, when all work on constructing the largest cathedral in all England was successfully completed, did not come until 1978. Sadly, Scott had died eighteen years earlier and so never saw his creation in its full glory.

The technical stuff

Length	619ft
Area	104, 275 sq/ft
Height of the tower	331ft
Choir vault	116ft
Nave vault	120ft
Under tower vault	175ft
Tower arches	107ft

There are 13 bells surrounding the bourdon bell 'Great George, which itself weighs over 14 tons.

THE METROPOLITAN ROMAN CATHOLIC CATHEDRAL

The Metropolitan Roman Catholic Cathedral (built between 1962 and 1967) is a beast of a very different nature. Both internally and externally it is modernistic and creates an impression very different from that of its Anglican counterpart. At first glance it does not look like a cathedral: in fact, at first glance it is very difficult to work out exactly what its function is and when it was first built its odd shape gave rise to epithets such as 'the Mersey funnel' and 'Paddy's Wigwam'. As it turned out, the revolutionary design was highly symbolic; the 'spiky' roof was meant to symbolise the crown of thorns and the circular interior is designed to encourage inclusivity. Traditional churches divide the congregation from the officiating clergy, but in the new cathedral there was no such

The Catholic cathedral.

dividing line. The priests became part of the congregation and the congregation was considered at one with the officers of the church. Whether or not intentionally, the amphitheatre at the centre of the design is a reminder of the early Christian church when Roman architecture would have formed a backdrop to many of the disciples' addresses and sermons.

There had been several attempts to design and build a cathedral to cater for Liverpool's Catholic community. In the 1930s Edwin Lutyens had produced an extremely ambitious design which seemed to owe more to the eastern branch of Christianity than that of the west. The part above ground never got off the drawing board, but construction did begin on the crypt, which is still there today as a base to the main body of the cathedral. When the building was completed there were those in the community who were a little surprised: many of the external features resemble what in traditional architecture is part of a building's skeleton – the concrete trusses, flying buttresses and a belfry which looks as if it is waiting to be hoisted aloft all create the impression of an edifice awaiting the final touches. The contrast with the Anglican cathedral at the other end of Hope Street could not be greater: one looks complete, traditional, solid and the other innovative, incomplete and even modernistic.

The technical stuff
Diameter: 195ft
13 side chapels
2 side porches
Central altar of solid marble 10ft long
The Great Organ has 88 stops and 4,565 pipes

Some facts
The architect for the Anglican cathedral was Catholic and the original architect for the Catholic cathedral, Sir Edward Lutyens, was Protestant.

Giles Gilbert Scott also designed the traditional red telephone boxes that used to grace our highways and byways.

He also designed the war memorial for St Nicholas's Church in Whiston on the outskirts of Liverpool. It was struck by lightning in 1928 and had to be replaced in 1932.

The marble for the altar in the Catholic cathedral was quarried in Skopje, Macedonia.

The Catholic cathedral also has more coloured glass as part of its design than any other cathedral in Europe.

THE ATHENAEUM

If you want to sample, or just observe, how the gentle folk of the days of yore lived in Liverpool all you have to do is visit the Athenaeum. This is a 'gentlemen's club' of the old style, with a news room and library furnished with leather armchairs and sumptuous carpets creating an ambiance more associated with Georgian or Victorian England than the age of the motor car, computer and interactive television. It is situated in Church Alley (off Church Street) and occupies three storeys, reached by way of an elegant elliptical staircase greeting the visitor or club member at the main entrance. The club was founded in 1797 (making it twenty-seven years older than the London club of the same name) by a group of Liverpool dignitaries which included the abolitionists James Currie and William Roscoe. Unlike many of the other architectural gems in Liverpool it is hidden away and could be easily missed by a passer-by; the only people likely to notice it are those who are deliberately seeking its whereabouts. Incidentally, the Athenaeum refers to those who join as 'proprietors', not members.

THE BLUECOAT CHAMBERS

The Athenaeum is not the only hidden masterpiece in this corner of the city. Literally just a few steps away, on School Lane, stands the beautiful example of Queen Anne architecture the Bluecoat Chambers, the oldest surviving building in Liverpool's centre, and probably the only building in the city which was originally built with purely charitable, altruistic intentions. Back in the early eighteenth century a kindly old sea captain, Bryan Blundell (1674–1756), was horrified at the sight of the many starving, destitute children he saw just about every day of his life as he walked through the city's streets. But unlike many of his contemporaries, who might also have been appalled at the abject poverty of the inhabitants of the city but did nothing about it, he decided he was going to make a difference. He could see no point in feeling pity for one's fellow man if that sympathy did not lead to some sort of action.

Bryan Blundell was a man of some means. He had been a part-owner of a trading ship and this had allowed him to amass a not inconsiderable fortune, part of which he was determined to put to good use. He teamed up with a certain clergyman, the Reverend Mr Stythe, in an attempt to alleviate the suffering of at least some of the local children. In 1718 the captain and the vicar opened a day school (later known as the Bluecoat School) and took 50 children off the streets, fed them and gave them a rudimentary education. Blundell also gave 10 per cent of his income to the running of the school and then set about brow-beating local businessmen into making whatever contribution they could afford in order to make the venture a success. When he died in 1756 the school was a thriving enterprise and, if he is looking down on us from a celestial cloud, he is no doubt delighted that his creation is still there today as Liverpool's last remaining grammar school, even if the school itself has moved out to Wavertree. Blundell's original building still survives but is now the Bluecoat Arts Centre.

THE LYCEUM

If the Athenaeum and the Bluecoat School are somewhat hidden from view, the same could not be said about another of Liverpool's elegant buildings. The lower end of Bold Street is dominated by the Lyceum, another example of how just how beautiful Liverpool's buildings can be. It was built in the early nineteenth century (it opened in 1802), and despite several attempts by Philistine planners to knock it down, still stands there with its majestic glory undiminished by the shops, cafés and fast-food establishments that surround it.

Like the Athenaeum, the Lyceum was originally built as a gentlemen's club-cum-reading room where the more educated members of Liverpool society could escape the hustle and bustle of everyday life. The increasingly popular but infinitely more rowdy coffee-houses were not to the taste of those who sought a more peaceful environment in which to catch up with the news and perhaps discuss business and the political developments of the day. Legend also has it that this is where many of the great and the good of Liverpool heard the news of Wellington's victory over Napoleon at Waterloo in 1815.

Shortly after opening, the Lyceum became the home of the first subscription library in the town. In 1803 it had about 2,000 volumes and by 1850 possessed no fewer than 37,000. It remained as a library until the Second World War. In the 1970s the council, unbelievably, gave permission for this beautiful old building to be demolished and the site to be developed as a shopping centre. Fortunately it was saved when Margaret Thatcher's government came to power, but who knows for how long?

LIVERPOOL ONE

In 2008 Liverpool was the European Capital of Culture. In the same year (and with the aid of a grant from the EU) Liverpool began its most ambitious building project since the end of the Second World War. Liverpool One, as it is now known, is just about as far, architecturally speaking, from the more traditional areas of the city as it is possible to be. The old Whitechapel and Paradise Street have been totally transformed. What used to be a rather dingy mixture of unattractive, poorly lit shops, an ugly concrete bus station and multi-storey car park, forlorn-looking patches of waste ground and some dwelling-houses which had seen better days in the dim and distant past, were swept away. In their place was erected a very modernistic selection of department stores, shops, cafés, high-rise apartments, restaurants, a 3,000-seater cinema and a 5-acre park.

Some facts

The total area of retail space in Liverpool One is just 1.8 million sq/ft.

The underground car park can hold up to 3,000 cars.

Restaurants offer diners the choice of food from all corners of the globe including: Mexican, Japanese, French, Italian, Portuguese, American, Thai, Chinese and Latin American.

THE ALBERT DOCK

In a city used to architectural transformation there is one transformation that comes as a bit of a shock: the Albert Dock. This nineteenth-century marvel of engineering and architectural ingenuity has enjoyed many incarnations, or reincarnations, even. At first it was, as the name suggests, a dock where the thriving port could unload tobacco, cotton, sugar, brandy, silk, etc. by the ton before they were transported to their destinations all over the country. There was, however, just one drawback. The dock was designed and built in the age of the old sailing

ships and when these started to be replaced by the bigger steam ships, the dock could not cope and so it had to change or die and it chose the former. It might not have been suitable for loading and unloading the new leviathans of the sea, but it was ideally placed for storing goods as they waited to be moved on elsewhere.

During the Second World War the dock took on another role. It was taken over by the Royal Navy and became a base for small warships, landing craft and submarines which formed part of the Atlantic Fleet. This, obviously, made the dock a target for the Luftwaffe and it was bombed on several occasions early in the war. During the post-war era the dock went into a seemingly irreversible economic decline and eventually, in 1972, the whole place was closed down. Its revival, when it came, was largely due to the riots which took place in Toxteth and shook the then Conservative government out of its complacency. Margaret Thatcher, desperate to see an end to the civil unrest in the city, dispatched Michael Heseltine northwards with instructions to do something about the blighted North-West. The solution he came up with was the creation in 1981 of the Merseyside Development Corporation. This august body of men decided that the best method of getting Liverpool off its knees would be to create jobs by renovating and regenerating the dock area and the result was impressive. In 1984 the International Garden Festival was opened which brought visitors in from all over the country and was generally hailed as a success. Part and parcel of this regeneration was the conversion of the old Albert Dock into a smart, up-market retail centre with shops, cafés, restaurants and hotels all centred around the old dock. In 1984 the 'gentrification' was increased when Granada Television took over the former Dock Office and then the process was completed when the flagship programme *This Morning*, hosted by Richard and Judy, was broadcast from the dockside studio.

Some facts
There is now a Beatles Museum on the Albert Dock, the only one of its kind in the world.

The Albert Dock was named after Queen Victoria's husband, Prince Albert Saxe-Coburg and Gotha.

The dock is now the home of the northern branch of London's Tate Gallery.

THE MUSEUM OF LIVERPOOL

It would be difficult to think of a building less like the traditional Three Graces than the new Museum of Liverpool. Opened in July 2011 it is a modernistic, not to say futuristic, architectural creation which now dominates Mann Island where not so long ago dismal pubs and run-down lodging houses reminded visitors of Liverpool's seafaring past. The new museum's design severs all connection with tradition and seems to say 'I am the future – bright and sleek yet at the same time functional and eco-friendly.' At first glance it resembles a film projected onto a screen in a cinema with its tapered central section and immense window looking out over the Pier Head. The Danish firm of architects 3XN who designed it certainly knew how to stop people in their tracks and take notice of their stunning creation which covers an area over 300ft long and 180ft wide.

The space-age looking museum on Mann Island.

Once inside visitors are treated to innovative and technologically state-of-the-art exhibitions and displays of the people and events that have played such an important role in the evolution of the city. The musty, dusty passive exhibits of the traditional museum are nowhere to be found; instead the accent is on interactive displays and the latest in visitor attraction technology. And all this is driven by a modern concept in museum design: interpretive displays are changed and refreshed regularly so that frequent visitors should expect to see something new every time they cross this amazing building's threshold.

Some facts
The building is covered with 5,700 sq m of stone cladding.

A Danish firm came up with the original design but then the project was handed over to the Manchester-based firm AEW to fill in the details.

When it opened in July 2011 there were more than 13,000 visitors on the first day.

LIVERPOOL UNIVERSITY

With all the additions and extensions this building has acquired over the years it is very difficult, if not impossible, to talk about it as a single building or architectural style. As it stands today it is either a pleasing amalgam reflecting the varying tastes of the architects involved in its creation, or it is a mish-mash of ill-conceived planning errors. The university as a whole really does confirm the old adage that beauty is in the eye of the beholder.

The original Victoria Building, constructed between 1889 and 1892, is monumental Gothic structure designed by Alfred Waterhouse and modelled on the traditional ideas of what an imposing, prestigious building should look like. The materials used in its construction were concrete, steel and the fiery Ruabon brick that gives it such a distinctive appearance.

When the establishment of a university in Liverpool was first discussed there were those among the business community who were not entirely enthralled by the prospect. Fortunately the more thoughtful members of the community eventually proved to be more persuasive and so, in 1881, a University College was founded and provision was made for students and lecturers to be accommodated at the top of Brownlow Hill. In 1884 the institution became part of the federal Victoria University, along with Owens College in Manchester, preparing students for the external examinations set and marked by London University. In 1903 Liverpool University College was awarded its own charter, conferring on it the status of an independent academic institution which could award its own degrees. It was now officially Liverpool University.

Some facts

The term 'red brick university' was coined by Edgar Allison Peers, professor of Spanish Studies from 1922 to 1952 at Liverpool University. He used the term in a book which he wrote under the pseudonym of Bruce Truscot.

The original Victoria Building stands on the site of disused lunatic asylum.

Liverpool University caters for just over 20,000 students of whom approximately 17,000 are undergraduates and 4,000 are post-graduates.

Some notable Liverpool University former students:

Steve Coppell	footballer	Economic History
Carol Ann Duffy	Poet Laureate	Philosophy
Sir Frank Kermode	academic	English
Ramsay Muir	historian	History
Phil Redmond	TV producer	Social Studies
Stella Rimington	Director General MI5	Archive Administration
Pat Arrowsmith	peace campaigner	Social Science
Tony McNulty	politician	Political theory and institutions
Jon Snow	broadcaster	Law
Chris Lowe	pop musician	Architecture
Barry Horne	footballer	Chemistry
Winifred Robinson	broadcaster	English
Patricia Routledge	actress	English

THE SUPERLAMBANANA

Anyone new to Liverpool enjoying a bit of shopping in and around the city centre might be a little surprised at one example of street sculpture which has made its appearance in various places over

the past 15 years. Standing an impressive 17ft high and weighing in at just a shade under 8 tons, the SuperLamBanana is not what a visitor to the city might expect to see. At first he or she probably thinks it is just a piece of fanciful nonsense or another example of wacky modern art. But in fact it does attempt to convey a serious message.

It was the brainchild of the US-based Japanese artist Taro Chiezo who was concerned about what he saw as the dangers of science getting out of hand. He was particularly worried about the unforeseen (or just ignored) possible consequences of genetic engineering and expressed his concerns by taking a banana and a lamb, both of which were traditionally imported and exported in great numbers through the port of Liverpool, and combining them, quite literally. The result was the SuperLamBanana as it exists today. So remember: it is not just fanciful rubbish; it is a warning of what might happen if we meddle too much with nature!

RODNEY STREET

There is something special about Rodney Street. It is known as the Harley Street of the north because it has so many eminent doctors' surgeries occupying its fine Georgian buildings. But it also has no fewer than sixty Grade II listed buildings and a Grade II listed church. Rodney Street also has associations with several famous people:

Born in Rodney Street:
Arthur Hugh Clough	(1819–61), poet
Anne Clough	(1820–92), suffragette
William E. Gladstone	(1809–98), Prime Minister
Nicholas Monsarrat	(1910–79), novelist
Brian Epstein	(1934–67), entrepreneur

Lived in Rodney Street:
E. Chambré Hardman	(1898–1988), photographer
William Roscoe	(1753–1831), philanthropist

The Hungarian Consulate is also in Rodney Street.

6

THE WORLD OF ENTERTAINMENT

Showbiz is crammed with Scousers. The only problem is that many young people think that entertainment in Liverpool started in 1963 with The Beatles, but this is not true. Long before the Fab Four were even a twinkle in their fathers' eyes, Liverpudlians were making people laugh or cry; encouraging them to sing or dance and making them feel terrified or moved to pity by what they were seeing portrayed on the stage or screen. And all tastes have always been catered for. High drama, pop music, classical music, farce and stand-up comedy have all found gifted exponents among those fortunate enough to have been born on the banks of the Mersey. Here are just a few of them:

COMICS

Arthur Askey

Born 6 June 1900, Arthur Bowden Askey was a tiny man (5ft 2ins) but was full of boundless energy and a seemingly endless sense of fun. He was educated at the prestigious Liverpool Institute grammar school and when he left he took a job as a junior clerk in the Liverpool Education Offices. But he soon discovered that this was not what he wanted to do for the rest of his life and, at the tender age of sixteen, packed in his clerical career and tried his hand in show business. He began by working in pubs and must have been reasonably successful as he remained an entertainer for the rest of his life. In the First World War he went off to entertain the troops and, when the war was over, returned to the stage.

The Liverpool Institute, now renamed the Liverpool Institute for Performing Arts.

In 1938 he was taken on by the BBC and, after striking up a partnership with Richard Murdoch, another comic, soon became a hit with the audiences. The duo soon became household names as 'Big-hearted Arthur and Stinky Murdoch'. When he died in 1982 he had been in the business for over sixty years, and, even at the end, could still raise the roof with his witty one-liners and brilliant ad libbing.

Jimmy Tarbuck OBE
Jimmy Tarbuck was born in Liverpool on 6 February 1940. He left school at fifteen and his first job was as an apprentice car mechanic. But his heart was not in the job and he was invited to seek employment elsewhere, mainly because of his propensity for fooling around. After a while he was taken on as a Butlin's Redcoat and this set him on the road to a very successful showbiz career. He burst onto our television screens in the 1960s, more or less at the same time as The Beatles. His trademark gappy

front teeth, ready wit and personal charm made him the obvious choice when TV producers were looking for someone to front variety shows such as *Live from the Palladium* and *Sunday Night at the London Palladium*. Away from the stage, 'Tarby' (as he is generally known) is a passionate sportsman; he is a firm supporter of Liverpool FC and an obsessive golfer. Strangely for a Garston boy he makes no secret of the fact that he votes Tory and famously baked a birthday cake for Margaret Thatcher on her sixtieth birthday.

Les Dennis

Another Garston lad, Les Dennis (real name Leslie Dennis Heseltine), was born on 12 October 1953, the son of a factory worker mother and father who, after leaving the Royal Navy in which he served in the war, became a clerk in a bookmaker's. Leslie was a bright lad at his infants' school and went on to pass the 11+ and win a place at Quarry Bank High School. But the life of an academic was not for him and while he was still at school he was attracted by the bright lights and began performing in the pubs and working men's clubs in the North-West. His chance to hit the big time came in 1974 when he won the ITV talent show *New Faces* and since then he has been a regular host of game shows on the telly. But he has also appeared in the theatre, in films, played several parts in television soaps and is a regular performer in pantomime all around the country at Christmas. He has been married three times and has found the time to write his autobiography, *The Show Must Go On*.

Faith Brown

Faith Brown, whose real name is Eunice Irene Carroll, was born in Liverpool in 1944 and decided at a very early age that the only career she was interested in was that of an entertainer. She had already set out as a singer at the age of fifteen and within a very short space of time was the resident singer at the Rialto ballroom (which was burned to the ground during the Toxteth riots of 1981). She later joined forces with her three brothers to form the group The Carrolls which released several records in the 1960s and enjoyed moderate success. But it is on her talent as a comedienne and impersonator that her reputation rests. She first came to the attention of the viewing public in ITV's *Who do you do?* (1975–6) and then was a regular participant in game shows such as *Celebrity Squares* (1975–9), the BBC's *Blankety Blank* (1979–90) and a host of other shows of similar ilk. In 2006 she spent 14 days in the jungle after agreeing to subject herself to all manner of masochistic trials in *I'm a Celebrity Get me out of Here!*

Stan Boardman

Born on 7 December 1940, Stan Boardman came into the world of entertainment by accident. He really wanted to be a professional footballer but, although a player of no mean ability, he was considered not quite good enough to make into the ranks of the professionals. As an alternative career he set up his own haulage business which helped him keep the wolf from the door. Then, in 1976, he went on a family holiday to Butlin's in Pwllheli, North Wales, where he was persuaded to take part in one of the camp's regular talent shows. Reluctantly he got on his feet and started telling jokes. The effect was immediate and within no time he had a packed house rolling in the aisles. Not surprisingly he won first prize (£1,000) and the rest, as they say, is history. But his career has not been without controversy and he has found himself in trouble on several occasions because of the perceived racist content of some of his jokes – 'the Germans bombed our chip shops' is one of his milder allusions to foreigners. Off stage he is still a keen sportsman, although nowadays golf occupies most of his free time. In fact his golf has taken him all around the world (Bangkok, South Africa, Germany, etc.) and he is rightly proud of his 15 handicap, which is not bad for an amateur.

Ted Ray

Born in Wigan on 21 November 1905, Charlie Olden (his real name) moved to Liverpool with his parents just a few days after he was born. His father was a comedian in the old music halls and young Charlie obviously had the smell of greasepaint in his nostrils all the time he was growing up. After a spell at 'normal jobs' such as working as a ship's steward and then an office clerk, he began his move into the world of entertainment. He had learned to play the violin as a boy and this gave him his entrée;

he was taken on as dance band violinist. Then, in 1927, he made his debut performance as a comic at the Palace Theatre in the Lancashire town of Preston and never looked back. By 1930 he was performing in London at the London Music Hall.

This was the time when radio and radio entertainers were starting to play an ever-increasing role in people's lives. They no longer had to go and queue for the theatre, music hall or cinema to be entertained: they could just turn the knob on the radio set and listen to whatever took their fancy. And Ted soon became part of this world. By 1949 he had his own radio show, *Ray's a Laugh* and later became a regular panellist on the long-running *Does the Team Think?* Unlike a lot of his contemporaries, Ted Ray made the transition to television without much trouble and in 1955 made regular monthly appearances on our screens in *The Ted Ray Show* (until 1958). But his talents did not stop there. The star of music hall, radio and television was also at home on the big screen and from the 1930s appeared in films such as *Elstree Calling* (1930), *Radio Parade of 1935* (1935) and *Carry on Teacher* (1959). He also found the time to write two autobiographical works: *Raising the Laughs* (1952) and *My Next Turn* (1963). He died in 1977.

Some facts
Charlie Olden 'borrowed' the name Ted Ray for his stage persona from a 1920s British (actually, born on Jersey) professional golfer.

In the early days one of Ted Ray's 'alter egos' was Nedlo, the Gypsy violinist. This was just his real name spelled backwards.

Ken Dodd OBE
To give him his correct, full title, Dr Kenneth Dodd OBE was born on 8 November 1927 in Knotty Ash, a suburb of Liverpool which he went on to make famous with his Diddy Men and the Knotty Ash jam butty mines. If prizes were given out for sheer longevity in the world of performing, Doddy (as he is generally known) would run away and leave the other contestants way behind. He is now in his eighties and has been entertaining the crowds for almost sixty years and, what is more, he shows no sign of wanting to slow down and take things a bit easier. Retirement is for other people;

he can still stand on stage and reel off jokes, indulge in repartee and make off-the-cuff quips that leave audiences clutching their sides with laughter. And while he can still do that he is not going to abandon the career which has been his whole life for well over half a century.

Ken Dodd was the son of a Liverpool coal merchant and, when he left school (he attended the Holt High School in Childwall), he worked for his dad for a while, but developed this funny idea that he wanted to become a ventriloquist. He spent 6d on a booklet which would help him master the art and then saved up to buy himself a dummy.

He began his career on the stage at the Nottingham Empire in 1954 and within four years was topping the bill in Blackpool. With his tickling stick and naughty sense of the ridiculous he can make the most banal situation appear humorous. He also likes to take people and institutions down a peg or two and can puncture pomposity with a few well-chosen words. On one occasion he dismissed Freud's academic assessment on the nature of humour by suggesting that the psychologist's problem was that he never had to play the Glasgow Empire on a Saturday night after Rangers and Celtic had both lost!

But there are other sides to Ken Dodd's seemingly endless list of talents. His acting ability has allowed him to take parts in Kenneth Branagh's production of *Hamlet* as well as playing Malvolio in the Royal Shakespeare Company's production of *Twelfth Night*. And his singing voice has provided a very different angle on his career: he has an 'easy listening' tenor voice and his records have sold in their millions; 'Tears' is one of the best-selling records of all time.

Some facts
Ken Dodd holds honorary doctorates from Liverpool Hope University and Chester University. He is also a Fellow of LJMU.

There is now a statue of him on Lime Street station.

Freddie Starr

Frederick Leslie Fowell was born in Huyton on 9 January 1943 and, according to his own account, had a pretty rough upbringing by a father who did not think twice about giving the young Freddie a severe beating. In his teens Freddie Starr, as he now called himself, was the lead singer in a group called The Midnighters who performed around Liverpool and the night spots of Hamburg at about the same time as The Beatles were starting to make a name for themselves. And just like The Beatles, the Midnighters were managed by Brian Epstein.

But it was not as a pop singer that Freddie made his name. He has a unique, madcap (some might say weird) sense of humour which can reduce an audience to fits of laughter in seconds. He had been entertaining audiences in northern pubs and clubs since the mid-1960s but first brought this side of his talent to the notice of the general public in the TV talent show *Opportunity Knocks*. He then appeared on *The Royal Variety Performance* in 1970 and from 1972 he was a stalwart on the ITV show *Who do you do?*

Much of his fame, however, rests on the now famous headline that appeared in the *Sun* newspaper: 'Freddie Starr Ate My Hamster'. The article went on to say that he had come home late one night and asked a friend's girlfriend to make him a sandwich. When she refused he is supposed to have picked up her pet hamster, put it between two slices of bread and taken a bite out of it. Of course the story was totally untrue – it was just a stunt dreamed up by the publicist Max Clifford who later admitted that the whole thing was a ruse to get Freddie Starr nationwide publicity. It certainly worked.

Some facts

Freddie's father was a bare-knuckle fighter.

Freddie owned the horse Miinnehoma which won the Grand National in 1994.

ACTORS AND ACTRESSES

Rex Harrison

Rex Harrison or, as he is correctly styled, Sir Reginald Carey Harrison, was born in Tarbock Road, Huyton (then in Lancashire, now a suburb of Liverpool), in 1908 and attended St Gabriel's infants' school on Ellis Ashton Street. After St Gabriel's he went on to the prestigious public school Liverpool College.

Despite being almost blind in one eye, as a result of catching measles when he was a child, Rex (he adopted the name because he knew it was the Latin for 'king') not only made a success of acting as a career, but was commissioned into the RAF during the war. At first he was rejected because of his visual impairment, but he persisted and was eventually accepted and given a ground job. As Flight Lieutenant Harrison he was given a desk job guiding damaged bombers to airfields where they could land safely on their return from bombing raids over Germany.

Rex Harrison first stepped onto the boards at the Liverpool Rep Theatre in 1924 although his debut was less auspicious than he probably hoped for; he forgot his line (yes, singular!). But he did not let this initial gaffe interfere with his career plan and he went on to win award after award and star in some of the major stage and screen productions of the twentieth century. He is probably best remembered for his performances in films such as *Blithe Spirit* (1945), *Cleopatra* (1963), *My Fair Lady* (1964), *The Agony and the Ecstasy* (1965) and *Dr Doolittle* (1967).

His adoption of the name Rex could not have been more fortuitous when it came to his private life. Perhaps he had some sort of premonition that he, like one of the most famous kings of England, would have six wives. 'Sexy Rexy's' were: Colette Thomas (1934–42), Lilli Palmer (1943–57), Kay Kendall (1957–9); Rachel Roberts (1962–71), Elizabeth Rees-Williams (1971–5) and Mercia Tinker (1978–90, when he died).

Some facts

Rex Harrison has a style of hat named after him.

He was a wine connoisseur but his favourite drink was Guinness stout.

He was knighted in 1989.

Leonard Rossiter

Had it not been for a German bomb in the Second World War, most of us would probably never have heard of Leonard Rossiter. His first career choice was to become a schoolmaster, but fate had a way of changing his plans.

He was born in Wavertree in 1926, the son of a barber, and the family lived over the shop. When war was declared Leonard's father enrolled as a part-time ambulance man. While he was out one night 'doing his bit' for the war effort he was killed in an air raid and this put paid to young Leonard's plans. At the time he was a pupil at the Liverpool Collegiate School where he displayed an aptitude for, and an interest in, modern languages. In fact his ability was such that he was offered a place at Liverpool University and he planned to graduate and then become a teacher. But the bomb that killed his father meant that he could not afford to take up the university place as he now had to support his mother. Had his father survived the war, young Leonard would almost certainly have gone on to qualify as a teacher of languages and then spent the rest of his life in some obscure school counting the days until he could draw his pension.

When the time came for him to do his National Service he served in Germany in the Education Corps and no doubt took the opportunity to brush up on his German at the same time. After demobilisation he returned to Liverpool and got a job as a clerk with the Commercial Union insurance firm and, although he stuck it for six years, no-one could ever say that his heart was really in his work. It was about this time that he developed an interest in amateur dramatics and discovered, right from the start, that he had a talent for it. His sense of timing, the ease with which he learned his lines and his distinctive use of facial expressions were spotted by producers and directors and Leonard was persuaded to turn pro. He gave up his day job and made his debut as a professional actor in Preston in 1954. When he broke into films his first role was as Mr Shadrack, the boss in *Billy Liar*, and pretty soon offers of works were coming in thick and fast. When he started work in television, audiences immediately appreciated his wit and unique style so that series such as *Rising Damp* (1974–8) and *The Fall and Rise of Reginald Perrin* (1976–9) will almost certainly go down in the history of the medium as examples of TV situation comedies at their very best.

Leonard Rossiter was a keen sportsman and keep fit fanatic who played football, squash and tennis. But he tragically dropped dead at the relatively young age of fifty-seven in 1984.

Jean Alexander

Anybody old enough to have been watching television in the 1960s will be well acquainted with Jean Alexander. She has graced our screens in a wide variety of guises since her debut into the medium in the long-running police series *Z-Cars*, first broadcast back in 1962. She was born Jean Alexander Hodgkinson in Toxteth on 24 February 1926 and after school became a library assistant. However, being surrounded by books day in day out was not for Jean. Since childhood she wanted to be an actress and made her debut on the stage in Macclesfield in 1949. Her innate talent for the stage was recognised right away and she was seldom out of a job and, once she had made it into TV, she literally had a job for life. She joined the cast of *Coronation Street* in 1964 as Hilda Ogden and, together with her stage husband Stan, provided the comedy element in the soap for twenty-three years. When she decided, in 1987, that she had nothing more to offer the show, she retired, but this did not mean that she disappeared from our screens. From being a somewhat bossy housewife in Salford, Jean was transformed into the money-grabbing proprietor of a clapped-out old junk shop in the Yorkshire Dales in what became another long-running favourite with the viewers, *Last of the Summer Wine*. As Aunty Wainwright she injected her unique brand of humour into what was already a very funny show which, in total, ran from 1973 to 2010.

Jean never married and, after a lifetime spent making an incalculable contribution to light entertainment, she retired to Southport where she lives quietly, but no doubt satisfied, as she looks back over her life, with a job well done.

Some facts

In 2005 Jean Alexander was voted 'The Greatest Soap Opera Star of All Time' in a poll organised by the *TV Times*.

No less a figure than Sir Laurence Olivier was a founder member of the Hilda Ogden Appreciation Society.

Tom Baker

To hear him speak, you would never guess it but Thomas Stewart Baker was born in 1934 of very poor parents in Scotland Road, once one of the most run-down areas of Liverpool. His sonorous voice is totally devoid of any of the sounds which are normally so difficult to eradicate from the Liverpool accent and which might have barred him from many of his acting roles. His father was a ship's steward (and hardly ever at home) and his mother combined working as a barmaid with earning a few coppers as a cleaner. At school Tom was, by his own admission, not very successful academically but he was interested in religion. And this, together with a little persuasion from his devout Catholic mother, led to consider the priesthood as a career. In fact, he became a monk for six years until he had a moment of what we might call reverse conversion; he lost all faith and walked out of the monastery never to return (literally and metaphorically). Tom once claimed that he and God 'were an item', but the relationship turned out not to be permanent. It was about this time that he took up acting as a serious hobby. In fact his hobby was so serious that he was accepted into Laurence Olivier's National Theatre and it was even through Lord Olivier's good offices that Tom got his big break into films. He was offered the part of the mad monk Rasputin in *Nicholas and Alexandra* (1971), a part for which he was admirably suited and one which he played with obvious relish. Other films in which he starred include *The Canterbury Tales* (1972) and the TV film *Frankenstein: the True Story* (1973).

In his career as an actor he has had many successes, but perhaps the role for which he is best remembered is that of Dr Who (of which character he was the fourth incarnation) in the TV series of the same name. He played the doctor from 1974 to 1981 and, in the opinion of many, was the best of all the actors who have taken on the role. When he first appeared on screen as the eccentric doctor he quickly caught the public's imagination. His impressive height and presence (he is 6ft 3in tall) together with his distinctive speaking voice (not to mention the enormously long scarf he used as a prop) endeared him to generations of *Dr Who* fans. And the distinctive speaking voice has stood him in good stead in other areas. In particular, it has provided him with what could be described as a parallel career; he is frequently in demand as a voiceover artist.

Some facts
Tom Baker was labouring on a building site when he was offered the part of Dr Who.

When interviewed on the *Richard & Judy* show he said that he reads the Old Testament because he enjoys 'cheap, lurid melodrama.'

His National Service was spent in the Royal Army Medical Corps (1955–7).

Alison Steadman OBE
Alison Steadman is one of the most versatile actresses this country has ever produced. From her portrayal of the dippy Candice Marie in *Nuts in May* (1976) to the seductive Beverly in *Abigail's Party* (1977) and the hysterical Mrs Bennet in *Pride and Prejudice* (1995), Alison Steadman has never failed to impress with her acting ability. She was born in Liverpool in 1946 and educated at Childwall Valley High School. None of her relatives had anything to do with the stage and when the time came for Alison to leave school, few guessed that she would eventually end up being referred to as a 'national treasure' on account of her undoubted

and varied talents. For several years after she left school she was employed by the Liverpool Probationary Service as a secretary. But taking shorthand and sitting behind a typewriter was not for Alison and, in her early twenties, she headed off down to London, determined to carve out a career for herself on the stage. And she certainly managed that; in fact she carved out a career on stage, in television and in films and just about everything she did in any medium was well received by audiences and critics alike. Her debut was in *The Prime of Miss Jean Brodie* at the Theatre Royal, Bath, in 1968, where she also went on to play Ophelia in *Hamlet* in the same year. Her list of film credits is also apparently endless, but perhaps her most memorable performances were as Jane in *Shirley Valentine* (1989) and Gwenda Stimpson in *Clockwise* (1986).

Some facts

Originally, Alison Steadman wanted to be an archaeologist.

Shirley Valentine was originally a play written by another Scouser, Willy Russell.

Her hobby is collecting coloured milk bottle-tops.

Patricia Routledge CBE

Patricia Routledge made a name for herself in musicals in America before she achieved fame in Britain. Katherine Patricia Routledge was born on 17 February 1929 in Birkenhead where her father owned a gentlemen's outfitters. The family lived over the shop – apart from during the air-raids in the Second World War when they all decamped down into the cellar which doubled as their own private shelter.

Patricia attended Birkenhead High School and in addition was a keen member of the local church choir and taught at Sunday school. After school she went on to become a student at Liverpool University where she read English language and literature. One might have expected an academically able student, as Pat obviously was, to turn to the world of academe in some form for a career, but no; Particia Routledge had decided that she wanted to go onto the stage and that is what she did. In fact, her determination and single-mindedness pushed her into working at the Liverpool Playhouse for no pay at all, until the 'powers that were' suddenly decided that she could join the company. Her acting debut was on the Playhouse stage in 1952.

Now that acting was in her blood she moved down to become a student at the Old Vic Theatre School in Bristol and from there moved on to the Liverpool Playhouse and then London. By 1966 she had moved over to America and was appearing on Broadway. She was a hit in Alan Bennett's *Talking Heads* in 1987, but the main role for which she is remembered in UK of course is as Hyacinth Bucket (which she insisted should be pronounced 'bouquet') in *Keeping up Appearances*, a TV show which enjoyed enormous success from the very first broadcast in 1990. In the programme she plays the archetypal middle-class housewife with ideas way, way above her station. She is convinced that she is one of society's *crème de la crème,* but her relatives and in-laws are a constant, and frequently unwelcome, reminder that her origins are really very humble.

Some facts
She was voted Britain's favourite actress in 1996.

Patricia is an honorary Doctor of Letters at Liverpool University.

She is reported to have said that when she dies and goes to heaven she wants to hear the champagne corks popping, an orchestra playing and her mother's voice.

She was awarded an OBE in 1993 and a CBE in 2004.

Daniel Craig
Daniel Wroughton Craig was born 2 March 1968 in Chester but spent much of his childhood in Liverpool and at school on the Wirral. His father had been in the Merchant Navy and when he decided to give up the seafaring life became, first of all, a steel erector and then took to managing a pub (the Ring o' Bells) just outside Frodsham. Daniel's mother contributed to the family finances by teaching art.

It was while acting in a school production of *Oliver!* that young Daniel, aged six, got the acting bug. Once he had experienced the adulation of an appreciative audience he never really considered any other career and, with his own inclinations enthusiastically encouraged by his mother, the teenage Daniel set off for the bright lights. He was accepted into the National Youth Theatre, but still had to make ends meet by working as a waiter when 'resting' from acting roles. It was at this point that he began trying to get into the Guidhall School of Music and Drama, but he first attempts were not successful. However, he persisted and his determination paid off. Then the offers began to come in and Daniel was finally on the road to being a box-office hit. Early film and television roles included *The Power of One* (1992) and *Our Friends in the North* (1996) but his big breakthrough came with *Lara Croft: Tomb Raider* (2001) and *Road to Perdition* (2002), after which he never looked back. In 2006 he played James Bond in *Casino Royale* and this was followed by *Quantum of Solace* in 2008, both of which received critical acclaim. Previous Bonds such as Sean Connery and Roger Moore were greatly impressed by 'the new boy'.

Some facts

Daniel Craig, at 5ft 11ins, is the shortest of the actors who have played James Bond.

He was paid over £6,000,000 for his first two Bond films.

His personal favourite Bond film is *From Russia with Love* which starred Sean Connery.

THE ALL-ROUNDERS

There are some Scousers in the world of entertainment who just cannot be pigeonholed. These are the ones who can do various combinations and permutations of singing, dancing, acting, painting, doing stand-up comedy, writing, playing musical instruments and even talking for hours with wit and authority that just leave the rest of us spellbound. Here are a couple.

George Melly

It is almost impossible to sum up the gifts, talents and abilities of a man like Alan George Heywood Melly in a few words. Bon viveur, raconteur, author, journalist, jazz singer, art critic and art historian, he was a closet intellectual and academic propelled through life by an enormous sense of fun and a determination to give his passions and interests unbridled freedom. With the outrageous fedoras and shocking zoot suits which he liked to wear, he cut a very distinctive figure on his local high street as much as on any stage. Only a man with as big a personality as George's would have had the *chutzpah* to get away with such sartorial inelegance.

Unlike many of his co-performers from Liverpool, George was born (in 1926) into a relatively well-off, middle-class family and spent his childhood in a large, Victorian house (with a nanny and servants) in the Sefton Park area of the city. His father was a businessman and his mother enjoyed mixing with the local 'luvvies' and prominent members of Liverpool society. When the time came he was packed off to Stowe public school (where boarding fees for 2010/11 are a shaving under £30,000 per year) in Buckinghamshire where he displayed an interest in the history of art and in particular Surrealism. These were interests which were to stay with him for the rest of his life and he wrote and lectured about them with penetrating insight for most of his adult life. On one particularly memorable occasion, when it had been announced to the world that George was suffering from dementia, he remarked that Alzheimer's disease was not such a bad thing for anyone interested in Surrealism!

In 1944 George joined the Royal Navy for no other reason than that he liked the bell-bottom trousers, but he was given his marching orders after a number of books which were considered to be subversive were found in his locker. Back in Civvy Street he drifted into the world of jazz and jazz musicians and eventually joined Mick Mulligan's Magnolia Band. By his own admission he was too lazy to learn how to play a musical instrument and relied on his singing voice. Fortunately this was not bad; he had a gruff voice which was admirably suited to imitating his idol, the American blues singer Bessie Smith.

When people started to lose interest in jazz and transfer their affections to the emerging rock 'n' rollers, George Melly turned to journalism and was the *Observer*'s music critic for several years. In 1974 he took the momentous decision to resign from the *Observer* and go back on the road. This was a bit of a gamble as pop music was still dominated by the groups who dreamed of becoming the new Beatles. But it was the right decision and, together with John Chilton and his Feetwarmers (and then Digby Fairweather), he packed the house out at every performance throughout the length and breadth of the land. And his popularity never waned. He died in 2007.

Some facts

When not raising hell George liked to get away from it all by fishing on the banks of the River Usk in South Wales.

He hated organised religion and was President of the British Humanist Association from 1972 to 1974.

He refused to accept a CBE.

Alexei Sayle

Another man of many parts, Alexei David Sayle was born in 1952 in Anfield to an English father and Jewish mother. Both his parents held very strong political views which veered to the extreme left. His name (which should be pronounced with the accent on the last syllable: Alexei) is Russian and is no doubt a reflection of his mother's admiration for the Russian dictator Joseph Stalin. Even as a youngster he did little to cover up his own strong political convictions and, after the student riots in Paris in 1968, became a card-carrying member of the British Communist Party.

Alexei received his secondary education at Alsop School, then one of the leading state-run grammar schools in Liverpool. He then proceeded to art college, first in Southport and then in Chelsea. It was while he was studying art in Chelsea that he got into stand-up comedy and shortly afterwards was performing at the Edinburgh Fringe Festival. From then on there was no turning back; his career was firmly marked out and he went on to expand and develop his talents in many fields. Television and radio soon proved a natural outlet for his anarchic humour and interest in the surreal and the absurd, not to mention his biting political satire. But the programme that was probably more responsible for bringing him to the attention of the British public than any other was *The Young Ones,* first broadcast in 1982, for which he wrote much of the material. The programme was violent, anarchic, and portrayed the life of students as absurd, aimless, feckless and grotesque, but it proved popular with the viewing public. At more or less the same time Alexei released his single *''Ullo, John! Gotta New Motor?'* which furthered his career as a satirist, but at the same time brought him a certain amount of notoriety as the song contained rather a lot of abusive and foul language which was not to everybody's taste. Nevertheless, it did not harm his career and he now expanded into the more serious side of film-making with roles in *Gorky Park* (1983), *Indiana Jones and the Last Crusade* (1989) and many more. Then, in 2008 he introduced the TV programme *Alexei Sayle's Liverpool,* a witty and thought-provoking look at his native city in which his original use of language and keen powers of observation found a natural medium for expression.

In 2010 Alexei published his autobiographical work *Stalin Ate My Homework,* a hilarious account of growing up as an only child with a gentle, polite father and rabidly Communist mother.

Some facts
Alexei Sayle has been an Honorary Professor at Thames Valley University since 1995.

He wrote a regular column for the motoring magazine *Car.*

When he was a boy, Alexei, his mum and his dad used to spend their holidays in what was then the Soviet Union.

LIVERPOOL HUMOUR:
EXAMPLE THIRTEEN

Overheard in a pub:

''Ello der gerl. Fancy a drink?'
'Oh ta. I'll 'ave a large gin and tonic with ice and lemon.'
'Two 'alves o' bitter over 'ere when yer ready, mate.'

7

THE MUSIC
MAKERS

It is impossible for people who did not experience the 1960s to appreciate just what it was like to be living in Liverpool at the time. Popular music and culture had been dominated by the Americans (Frank Sinatra, Johnny Ray, Doris Day, Elvis Presley and scores of others), then suddenly it all changed. Seemingly overnight, the centre of the universe moved to the banks of the Mersey where a sudden, and largely unexplained, explosion of creativity blew the city away and sent shockwaves all over the world. Beatlemania and the Merseybeat had arrived and the world of light entertainment was transformed. This is the official view. But what historians of popular music tend to forget is that Liverpool bred successful pop idols before the 1960s, even if they are now remembered only by the old and bold, the pop fanatics and the social historians. Let's have a look at some:

PRE-1963

Michael Holliday
Born Norman Alexander Milne on 26 November 1924, brought up in Kirkdale and blessed with a sonorous, treacle-smooth baritone voice he was usually billed as a crooner. Comparisons were often made between his voice and Bing Crosby's and singing style and the Old Groaner himself was very impressed by the boy from Liverpool. He had hits with 'The Yellow Rose of Texas' (1955), 'The Story of My Life' (1958) and 'Starry Eyed' (1960). Other songs he recorded did not enjoy the same success but were

nevertheless very popular at the time: 'Nothin' to Do' (1956), 'Hot Diggity' (1956), 'Stairway of Love' (1958). His last recording was 'Little Boy Lost' (1960). Unfortunately Michael suffered from emotional problems which, allied to the troubles he was having with the tax man, proved too much and he committed suicide at the age of thirty-eight on 9 October 1963. He is buried in Anfield cemetery.

Some facts
Michael Holliday always suffered from stage fright.

He wasn't 'discovered'. After winning a few talent contests he wrote to the BBC in December 1954 and asked for an audition.

Lita Roza
Born Lilian Patricia Lita Roza in Garston on 14 March 1926, Lita was one of the first of the post-war singers who came to dominate the 'hit parade' when the country was recovering from the effects of the war. And not many people today, even in Liverpool, appreciate the impact Lita Roza had. With her sultry good looks, no doubt inherited from her Spanish father, and tuneful voice she knocked up a couple of firsts: she was the first female singer to top the charts in Britain and she was the first singer from Liverpool to reach number one. And the song that brought her these successes was 'How Much is That Doggie in the Window?' which she recorded in 1953. Other songs which brought her varying degrees of success included 'Allentown Jail' (1951), 'Let me go, Lover' (1955), 'Hernando's Hideaway' (1955) and 'Oh dear, What Can the Matter be?' (1959). She died on 14 August 2008.

Some facts
Lita Roza hated the song that brought her fame and wealth, 'How much is that Doggie in the Window?'

Margaret Thatcher once admitted that, when she was a child, this was her favourite song.

Billy Fury

Billy Fury was born Ronald William Wycherley in Liverpoo on 17 April 1940 l and grew up in Garston in a working-class family who were well acquainted with the meaning of the word poverty. Billy himself worked on the docks and tug-boats until his pop-star good looks and singing voice (he has been described as a cross between Elvis Presley and James Dean) brought him to the notice of the local impresarios. His short career brought him the strangest of accolades: he is the most successful singer in the history of pop never to have had a number one hit. The highest he ever achieved was with 'Jealousy' in 1961, which went to number two and 'Halfway to Paradise' which hit the number three spot in the same year. Previously he had had varying degrees of success with his singles 'Maybe Tomorrow' (1959), 'Angel Face' (1959) and 'Wondrous Place' (1960).

In a sense there was something very ironic about his choice of stage name. Billy Fury was anything but 'furious' and in fact had a very caring, gentle side to him. As soon as he could afford it

Tribute to Billy Fury at the Pier Head.

he bought a farm in a remote part of mid-Wales where he cared for injured animals, particularly birds. He died of a heart attack at the cruelly young age of forty-two on 28 January 1983. In his memory Liverpool Council have erected a statue of him, with arms outstretched in a typically theatrical pose, at the Pier Head.

Some facts
His song 'Wondrous Place' was used as a the background music by the Toyota car manufacturers for some of their adverts in 1990 and 2000.

In 1994 the BBC broadcast a play based on his life. It was titled *The Sound of Fury*.

Frankie Vaughan
According to the story which Frank Abelson himself used to relate, the stage name Vaughan was suggested to him by his grandmother's pronunciation of the word 'one'. She was a Russian Jew who spoke English with a heavy accent and when she said 'Frank, you are a one' it sounded like 'you are a vorn' and 'vorn' became Vaughan.

Frank Abelson was born quite close to Liverpool city centre on 3 February 1928, the son of an upholsterer and a seamstress. He sang in the choir of the local synagogue and attended the local schools (Prescott Street and then the Harrison-Jones School on West Derby Street). After secondary school he studied art and eventually became an art teacher. While he was earning a living teaching art his singing talent was spotted by a BBC producer who painted a glowing future for him if he ever decided to turn professional. When he did take the plunge he was an instant success: in January 1957 he had a number one with 'The Garden of Eden'. This was followed by 'Tower of Strength' (1961) and a number of records which did not reach the number one spot, but which nevertheless did reasonably well: 'Give me the Moonlight' (1955), 'Green Door' (1956) and 'Kisses Sweeter than Wine' (1957). His last recording was 'When Your Old Wedding Ring Was New' (1987). Frankie Vaughan was also awarded the OBE in 1965 and the CBE in 1996 in recognition for the work he had done fostering boys' clubs. He died on 17 September 1999.

Some facts

Frankie Vaughan was a keen amateur boxer and at one time considered turning pro.

He was appointed Deputy Lord-Lieutenant for Buckinghamshire in 1993.

His nickname was 'Mr Moonlight'.

POST-1963

This was when the old world ended and the new world began. Once the Liverpool groups burst onto the scene nothing was ever the same again. The crooners, the jazz bands, the big bands and just about everybody else who earned a living either by singing or playing a musical instrument was faced with a choice: change or die (or, at least retire and grow vegetables). But contrary to popular belief the very first Liverpool group to break the new 'sound barrier' was not The Beatles; they were beaten to first place by Gerry and The Pacemakers (another of Brian Epstein's protégé groups) by just a few weeks. On 11 April 1963 they released 'How Do You Do It?' which shot right to number one. The Beatles' 'From Me to You' (composed by Lennon and McCartney on a coach as they travelled down to Shrewsbury for a gig) did not achieve this until 4 May.

Gerry and The Pacemakers

During the 1960s Gerry and his group were the only serious rivals to The Beatles. In fact Gerry and The Pacemakers achieved what no other band achieved for over twenty years: their first three releases went straight to the number one slot.

Gerry Marsden (real name Gerrard) was the son of Fred and Mary Marsden and he was born in the Toxteth area of Liverpool on 24 September 1942. From a very early age he knew what he wanted to do when he grew up: be a singer. When he was a mere five years old he sang a song for a group of appreciative adults and was so carried away by the applause that it was only ever going to be a matter of time before he was singing professionally. He attended Our Lady of Mount Carmel primary school on North Hill Street (it's still there) and, when he was old enough, joined a youth club where he learned to play the guitar and to box.

He first tried his hand at what was known as 'skiffle' and the people he gathered around him for this later transmogrified into The Pacemakers. The original line-up was Les Chadwick (bass guitar), Gerry Marsden (guitar), Freddie Marsden (drums) and Les McGuire (piano.)

Brian Epstein recognised Gerry and The Pacemakers' talent and signed them up in 1962. Success was immediate and in 1963 alone they had three chart-toppers: 'How Do You Do It?' (April), 'I Like It' (June) and 'You'll Never Walk Alone' (October). The last song was soon adopted by Liverpool Football Club as their anthem and can be heard even today at almost any Reds match. In 1964 the group released 'Ferry Cross the Mersey' which was an immediate chart-topper and became their signature tune.

Sadly, however, the group did not stay the course. Gerry and The Pacemakers, like every group except The Beatles, began to feel the winds of change blowing over the pop world at the end of the 1960s and decided to disband. A reconstituted group was formed in the 1970s which carried on through the 1980s and beyond, reliving some of the original group's successes, but never quite matching the magic of the glory days.

The famous Mersey ferry as immortalised by Gerry and The Pacemakers.

Some facts
Gerry and The Pacemakers were originally called Gerry and The Mars Bars but had to change it when the chocolate manufacturers complained.

Gerry Marsden was awarded an MBE in 2003 and made an Honorary Fellow of JMU in 2010.

In his youth Gerry did a bit of amateur boxing and one of his sparring partners was Alan Rudkin who went on to become a world-class bantamweight.

The Beatles
One characteristic separates The Beatles from all the other groups doing the rounds at the time: durability. More than all of their rivals they have demonstrated a certain *je ne sais quoi* which has guaranteed their survival as popular entertainers and ensured their place in musical history up there among the most influential creative geniuses of all time. Not bad for four young lads from Scouseland.

How this came about owes more to pure chance than skilful planning and if we want to trace the history of the band back to its very beginning we have to take ourselves back to a church garden fête in Woolton in 1957. John Lennon and Paul McCartney had never met, even though they lived only about 3 miles from each other. John Lennon was at St Peter's with his group The Quarrymen as they had been invited to provide the music for the church dance in the evening. Paul and John got chatting and found that they shared an interest in the popular music of the day. But that was not all; Paul had brought his guitar and gave John and his group a virtuoso demonstration of what he could do with it and they were impressed. In fact they were so impressed that they later invited him to join them as a guitarist.

From that moment in the grounds of St Peter's Church, history was in the making; the essential elements had come together which were to fuse into one of the most amazing phenomena in the whole history of popular culture. By 1960 The Quarrymen had had their day. A couple of members left and John Lennon, the group's founder and inspiration, had left school and moved on to pastures new, otherwise known as the Liverpool College of Art. It was here that he came into contact with another music fanatic,

Stuart Sutcliffe, who was immediately absorbed into another embryonic band Lennon was trying to form. Stuart suggested a name for the group: The Beetles (by analogy with an American group, The Crickets) which was adopted, early in 1960, but with a slightly different spelling: The Beetals. But John was still not entirely convinced. He knew they were on the right track but the name was not quite what he thought they were looking for. They tried 'Johnny and the Moondogs' then 'Long John and The Beatles' and even 'The Silver Beetles'. They finally decided, in August 1960, that the name they would adopt was The Beatles.

At this point there were five members of the group: John Lennon, George Harrison, Paul McCartney, Stuart Sutcliffe and the drummer Pete Best. Stuart Sutcliffe, however, soon decided that he wanted to leave the group and then, at the tragically young age of twenty-one, suddenly died of a brain haemorrhage. Pete Best was unceremoniously sacked because he was simply considered not good enough. He was replaced by Richard Starkey (aka Ringo Starr) and so the five were reduced to what was soon to be known worldwide as 'the fab four' . . . but not just yet. For the next eighteen months The Beatles honed their art providing the music for seedy strip-joints of Hamburg before they came home and were discovered by Brian Epstein. He took them in hand, told them to tidy themselves up and look more like professionals than the scruffy amateurs who were ten-a-penny in the pubs and clubs of Liverpool. Now they were ready to take over the world and that is exactly what they did.

From their very first release in 1962 until the group split up in 1970 The Beatles dominated the charts all over the world with unforgettable songs such as :

1962	'Love Me Do'
1963	'I Want to Hold Your Hand', 'Please Please Me', 'From Me to You', 'She Loves You'
1964	'A Hard Day's Night', 'I Feel Fine', 'Can't Buy Me Love', 'All My Loving', 'Twist And Shout'.
1965	'We Can Work It Out', 'Ticket to Ride', 'Help', 'Yesterday'
1966	'Paperback Writer', 'Yellow Submarine', 'Eleanor Rigby'
1967	'All You Need Is Love', 'Hello, Goodbye', 'Strawberry Fields Forever', 'Penny Lane'
1968	'Hey Jude', 'Lady Madonna'
1969	'The Ballad of John and Yoko', 'Get Back'
1970	'Let It Be', 'The Long and Winding Road'

They not only produced records, they also appeared in films which included:

1964	*A Hard Day's Night*
1965	*Help!*
1967	*Magical Mystery Tour*
1968	*Yellow Submarine*
1970	*Let It Be*

Some facts
Paul McCartney is left-handed but plays a re-strung, right-handed guitar.

When Ringo Starr was invited to join The Beatles he was the drummer for the group Rory Storm and The Hurricanes.

Stuart Sutcliffe was the only member of the group who was not a Scouser. He was born in Edinburgh in 1940.

Time magazine included The Beatles in their list of the world's 100 most influential people of the twentieth century.

The recording company Decca made what has to be one of the greatest mistakes of all time. They refused The Beatles a recording contract in 1962 stating 'We don't like their sound, and guitar music is on the way out.'

Ringo Starr came up with the phrase 'It's been a hard day's night' which provided the title for the song and the film.

Liverpool's airport, which used to be known as Speke Airport, was renamed John Lennon Airport in 2002.

IMMORTALITY RUSSIAN STYLE

In September 2011 in the Siberian town of Tomsk the authorities are planning to recreate the famous picture of The Beatles crossing Abbey Road. The idea is to reproduce the scene with life-size sculptures of John, Paul, George and Ringo 'crossing' a specially laid out zebra crossing close to one of Tomsk's main thoroughfares.

SOME OTHER HOPEFULS

In Liverpool in the early 1960s there were something in the region of 300 groups all trying to achieve fame and fortune. Most fell by the wayside, none came anywhere near to matching The Beatles, and some enjoyed limited success for a brief time. Here are some whose star burned brightly but then fizzled out:

Faron's Flamingos
Trevor Morais (drums), Paddy Chambers (guitar), Nick Crouch (guitar/vocals), William 'Faron' Ruffley (bass guitar/lead).

The Dennisons
Eddie Parry (vocals), Steve McLaron (lead guitar), Ray Scragge (rhythm guitar), Alan Willis (bass guitar), Clive Hornby (drums – Clive Hornby switched to acting and played Jack Sugden in *Emmerdale* from 1980 until his death in 2008).

The Big Three
Johnny Gustafson (bass guitar), Johnny Hutchinson (drums/vocals), Brian Griffiths (lead guitar/vocals).

Kingsize Taylor and The Dominoes
Ted Taylor (lead guitar/vocals), Sam Hardie (piano), Dave Lovelady (drums), Bobby Thompson (bass guitar), John Frankland (rhythm guitar).

The Kubas
Roy Morris (lead guitar), Stu Leithwood (rhythm guitar), Keith Ellis (bass guitar), Tony O'Reilly (drums).

The Swinging Blue Jeans
Ralph Ellis (guitar/vocals), Ray Ennis (lead guitar), Les Braid (bass guitar), Norman Kuhlke (drums)

Rory Storm and The Hurricanes
Alan Caldwell aka Rory Storm (vocals), Charles O'Brian (lead guitar), Johnny Byrne (rhythm guitar), Wally Eymond (bass guitar), Richard Starkey aka Ringo Starr (drums).

Freddie Starr and The Midnighters
Freddie Starr (vocals), Dave Garden (lead guitar), Johnny Kelman (rhythm guitar), Brian Woods (bass guitar), Keef Hartley (drums).

THE SEARCHERS

After The Beatles and Gerry and The Pacemakers, The Searchers were arguably the most successful of the 1960s Liverpool groups. They formed in 1960 (the original members being John McNally, Mike Pender and Tony Jackson with Norman McGarry on the drums) and for a few years were in great demand in and around the 'Pool. They performed regularly at The Iron Door Club and The Cavern and, for a while, were considered serious rivals to The Beatles for the top spot. They had several chart successes which included 'Sweets for My Sweet' (1963), 'Sugar and Spice' (1963), 'Needles and Pins' (1964), 'Don't Throw Your Love Away' (1963),

'Someday We're Gonna Love Again' (1964) and 'Love Potion Number Nine' (1964). Since the 1960s there have been several changes to the group's line-up, and one of the original members – Tony Jackson – has passed away, but The Searchers still tour the club circuit and perform to a loyal band of admirers and fans.

THE CAVERN WALL OF FAME

On Mathew Street, forming a backdrop to the statue of John Lennon, there is a so-called 'wall of fame' where each brick bears the name of the groups that performed at The Cavern between the years 1957 and 1973. The wall was unveiled by Gerry Marsden (lead singer with Gerry and The Pacemakers) in 1997. But it is not only those groups who made it to fame and fortune whose names appear here; some of the 'also rans' are also featured:

The Beatles (named individually John, George, Paul and Ringo)
The Who
Gerry and The Pacemakers
The Searchers
The Hollies
The Rolling Stones
The Manfreds
The Animals
Freddie and the Dreamers
The Temptations
The Mojos
The Fables
The Balloons
The Outcasts
The Astrals
The Pitiful
Warhorse
Gerry deVille and the City Kings
The Mojos
The Tempests
The Hardware
The Green Finger Four
The Blues Syndicate

Peaceful Nature
The Jazz Hatters
The Victors
The TT's
Steve Brett and the Mavericks
Wild Mouth
Guthries Klokke
The Jason Hertz Quintet
Good Habits
The Family
Gus Travis & the Midnighters

SETTING THE RECORD STRAIGHT

It all started with The Beatles at The Cavern, didn't it? Well no, not really. In the first place The Beatles were only one of a number of groups playing on Merseyside at the time and they definitely did not start by performing at The Cavern. There was another venue in Liverpool at the time called The Iron Door Club on Temple Street (off Dale Street and just a few minutes' walk from Mathew Street) which can rightly claim to be the birthplace of the Mersey Sound. Most of the big names performed there (The Beatles, Cilla Black, Gerry and The Pacemakers, etc.) before they picked up their guitars and drums and marched round the corner to The Cavern.

On 9 April 2005 a blue plaque was unveiled on the very spot where The Iron Door Club had once stood and part of it reads: 'The Beatles' (as The Silver Beetles) first show here 15 May 1960.' Brian Epstein did not 'spot' them at The Cavern until 9 November 1961.

AND WHAT ABOUT THE GIRLS?

Ask just about anyone to name a famous female singer from Liverpool and the answer is almost sure to be Cilla Black. And this is perfectly understandable as Cilla's fame, fortune and subsequent career has run parallel with The Beatles since she first stepped out of the cloakroom in The Cavern (where she was a hat-check girl) and belted out a song that impressed everybody in the audience, including Brian Epstein. But she was not the only one. There were other girls who dreamed of stardom and almost made it to the big time, only to find that, despite their undoubted talent, they were just not going to make it.

Cilla Black OBE

Cilla Black, who was born Priscilla Maria Veronica White on 27 May 1943 in the Scotland Road area of Liverpool is, of course, one of the most successful singers this country has ever produced. In the early days she was heralded as 'the new Gracie Fields' but went on to dominate the pop world in a way which Gracie could only have dreamed of.

Priscilla White attended St Anthony's primary and secondary school and then went on to Anfield Commercial College, no doubt assuming that her future, like so many girls' futures in those days, would be defined by her typing and shorthand speeds. But the gods had other plans for this girl from a deprived area of Liverpool. Her own inclinations were towards a career in showbiz and so she spent much of her spare time in the cloakroom of The Cavern jazz club, rubbing shoulders with some of the future big names on the Liverpool pop scene.

The first people to spot her potential were none other than John Lennon and Paul McCartney, who went so far as to write a couple of songs specifically for her. Then they introduced her to Brian Epstein who was not all that impressed at first. Then he suddenly spotted something in her and realised that he had a future star on his hands. From that moment there was no looking back for Miss White. In early 1964, as Cilla Black, she released 'You're My World' and 'Anyone Who Had a Heart'. Both records went straight to the number one slot.

Her success as a solo singer in the 1960s was phenomenal; everything she did as a singer seemed to turn to pure gold. Then, in the 1970s, she branched out into films, panto and made the first tentative steps in what was to be a very successful career in television. Then, at the age of forty-one, in 1984 she began hosting the programme *Surprise, Surprise* in which unsuspecting members of the public suddenly found themselves catapulted into the TV limelight and talking on camera to Cilla. The show was an instant hit with the viewers but Cilla Black was not one to rest on her laurels. Within no time at all she was hosting another show, *Blind*

Date, which turned out to be an even bigger hit with the public. As the title suggests, it involved getting a 'victim' on stage and selecting one of three other contestants for a date without seeing them first. The show proved spectacularly popular and kept 'our Cilla' on our screens for another eighteen years.

In her most recent incarnation (2011) Cilla Black has been making guest appearances on the long-running magazine show *Loose Women*. Her acid wit and unmistakable accent are still a source of entertainment, just as they were nearly fifty years ago when she first performed at The Cavern.

Some facts
She changed her name from White to Black after a journalist made a simple mistake and confused the colours! Cilla actually liked the change and adopted it.

Her mother had a second-hand clothes stall in St John's Market in the city centre.

Beryl Marsden
Beryl who? You might well ask! Beryl Marsden is probably the best of the 1960s pop singers who never quite made it. She was born Beryl Hogg in Toxteth in 1947 and for a brief time was one of the most popular singers in Liverpool. She was small, fiery but with a powerful voice and a great feeling for what an audience wanted to hear. She performed with some of the best (The Beatles, Rod Stewart, etc.) and released a few songs which, despite being as good as anything which was achieving at least moderate success at the time, never hit the charts. She had everything (the voice, the looks, the bubbly personality and even the contacts) but just seemed to lack the magic ingredient: luck.

Tiffany
Tiffany, the stage name of Liverpool-born Irene Green, was a 5ft 4in powerhouse of a singer who, in the 1960s, displayed all the signs of becoming one of the most successful singers of the era. She began her singing career by fronting the all-girl group The Liver Birds then made a career move and joined four lads who called themselves The Four Dimensions. The group became

Tiffany's Dimensions and for a while it looked as if they had a brilliant career to look forward to. But, unfortunately, fate had a nasty surprise in store for them. While they were travelling from venue to venue in Scotland their van and almost £3,000 worth of equipment were stolen – an enormous amount to lose in those days (to someone on an average salary this would have represented over three years' work). The group had no option but to return to Liverpool and consider their future, but, in reality, they had few choices open to them and the theft meant that they had reached the end of the road. Tiffany herself tried to branch out as a solo singer but her attempts were not crowned with glory. She released two singles in 1965 'Am I Dreaming?' and 'I Know' (which had also been released by Beryl Marsden). Neither made any impact on the buying public and, sad to tell, the same fate befell her next releases 'Find Out What's Happening' and 'Baby Don't Look Down'.

THE OTHER END OF THE SPECTRUM

Liverpool has earned such a reputation for popular culture over the past half-century that it is easy to forget that Scousers have also made a contribution to classical music. St George's Hall was built primarily to cater for the wealthy music lovers among the merchant classes and the Royal Philharmonic Hall was also built to cater for the more enlightened Liverpolitans of the day. And two individuals whose contribution to classical music on a worldwide scale hail from Liverpool: Sir Thomas Beecham and Sir Simon Rattle.

Sir Thomas Beecham
Sir Thomas Beecham was born on 29 April 1879 in St Helens. His father was unbelievably rich, having inherited the family business which was centred on the manufacture and sale of simple cures for common medical conditions: 'Beecham's Little Liver Pills' were supposed to relieve all the unpleasantness of constipation and 'Beecham's Powders' fought off colds and 'flu. While Thomas was still just a young boy the family moved to Huyton where the seemingly endless flow of cash into the family coffers meant

that as Thomas grew up he could indulge his every whim and passion without so much as a by-your-leave. Then, when the time came for him to be educated he was packed off to the prestigious and expensive Rossall public school in Lancashire, where the education he received would have been unashamedly upper class and traditional. After Rossall young Thomas went up to Wadham College, Oxford, but soon discovered that what Oxford had to offer was not what he wanted. By this time he had developed a passionate interest in music and, although he had never been trained as a musician, he set his mind (and heart) on a musical career. So he left Oxford for good to make his mark as a musician. This was a brave move for someone who was basically just a very gifted amateur, but his gamble paid off.

In 1899, largely just for his own pleasure and amusement, he established an amateur orchestra in St Helens. But, unbelievably, he turned out to be so good at his 'hobby' that in the same year he was conducting no less an august body than the Hallé Orchestra in Manchester. His reputation as a musician grew and grew and by 1910 he had moved to London where he found himself directing all the creative activities associated with Covent Garden. By the outbreak of the First World War he was renowned throughout Europe for his talent as a conductor and for his organisational skills.

Thomas Beecham was knighted in 1916 for services to British music. His enthusiasm for his art, however, got the better of him for a while and, despite being able to draw on the family's huge financial reserves for his extravagant projects, he found himself in serious trouble and was declared bankrupt in 1920. But Sir Thomas was not a man to be beaten and within a relatively short time he had recovered and was developing his career even further. By 1928 he was a guest conductor with the New York Philharmonic Orchestra and four years later, in 1932, founded the London Philharmonic Orchestra.

After the Second World War, which he spent mainly in America, Sir Thomas returned to England where he established the Royal Philharmonic Orchestra in 1946. He was the guiding spirit of the 'Royal Phil' until he was forced by ill health to lay down his baton in 1960. He died in London in 1961.

Liverpool Philharmonic Hall. It was officially opened with a concert conducted by Sir Thomas Beecham on 19 June 1939.

Some facts
Beecham was famous for his acerbic wit and contemptuous attitude to those less gifted than himself.

He once said that brass bands were alright in their place, by which he meant out of doors and several miles away.

Generally speaking he disliked English composers. Frederick Delius was probably the only one for whom he had any respect.

'I have just been all round the world and have formed a very low opinion of it' is one of his famous quotes.

On hearing that Sir Malcolm Sargent had been shot at in Palestine he quipped that he 'had no idea that the Arabs were so musical.'

Sir Simon Rattle
Sir Simon Rattle was born on 19 January 1955 in the Sefton Park area of Liverpool. He showed a very early interest in music, to the delight of his mother who encouraged and supported him enormously in his endeavours to become a professional musician. He attended Liverpool College where he was able to develop his

musical interests and learned to play piano, violin and percussion. But he had other cultural interests as well and when he went up to Oxford it was to study English Literature rather than music. Even now, when music has taken over as the dominant cultural interest in his life, his passion for literature has not deserted him. Writers such as Andrew Marvell and the sixteenth-century Spanish novelist Cervantes can help him unwind after a difficult day with the orchestra.

In 1974 Simon Rattle was appointed assistant conductor with the Bournemouth Symphony Orchestra. This was then followed by a stint as Assistant Conductor with the Royal Liverpool Philharmonic Orchestra, after which artistic triumphs and honours followed thick and fast. He made his debut as a conductor with the Berliner Philharmoniker Orchestra in 1987. This was a tremendous achievement by itself and one for which most career-minded musicians would die for, but in Simon's case it was followed by an even greater accolade. In 2002 he was appointed the orchestra's Chief Conductor, a position he still holds today.

Some facts
He began playing with the Merseyside Youth Orchestra when he was only ten years old.

His musical interests might be predominantly 'highbrow' but he also has a passion for Venezuelan dance music and is a particular fan of the Cuban jazz pianist Gonzalo Rubalcaba.

He was knighted in 1994.

LIVERPOOL HUMOUR: EXAMPLE FOURTEEN

Why wasn't Jesus born in Liverpool?
'Cos God couldn't find a virgin or three wise men.

8

SPORTS MAD

FOOTBALL

In Liverpool football is not a game; it's a religion. Anfield and Goodison Park are not football grounds; they are temples to the great Gods of the Pitch who are worshipped every Saturday afternoon (and more often if the devotees get a chance). These are occasions when the faithful congregate to sing hymns (the best known being 'You'll Never Walk Alone') and partake of a communion libation – usually a pint or three in a local hostelry before devotions commence. During the match 30–40,000 votaries stare fixedly at the vast altar on which the twenty-two human beings sacrifice themselves to one cause: total victory over the foreign gods.

And of course these gods, foreign or home-grown, don't come cheap. Managers pay millions in the hope of acquiring the services of a deity who will lead them gloriously to one of the twenty-first-century versions of the Holy Grail: the FA Cup, the Premiership or some equally coveted earthly reward. And the deities themselves are showered with riches beyond the dreams of avarice in the hope that they will bring the power and the glory to their team. If they succeed in doing this the pride and the passion of their religiously fanatical supporters are evident for all to see. If they do not, they suffer the verbal equivalent of a biblical stoning. They might be gods, but they can still suffer the wrath of the disappointed multitudes.

However, it was not always like this. In the early days football was nothing more than an enjoyable way for lads, many of whom did not have two pennies to rub together, to relieve the stresses and strains of the daily grind. It was not till the latter half of the nineteenth century that things got organised. And this meant change.

EVERTON FC

1878

This is usually taken as the start-date for football in Liverpool. History has it that the lads from St Domingo's Methodist Church in Everton thought that it might not be a bad idea to get a team together. They had been having their regular (or, more probably, irregular) kickabouts for years and decided in 1877 that it was time to formalise things a bit. So they formed a team and called themselves St Domingo's FC. Then, a year down the line, they changed the name to Everton FC and we all know the rest.

1888

When the Football League was formed in 1888 Everton FC was among the first teams in the country to join. And it was not long before they were beginning to make their mark. In fact they were so good that they won the League Championship in 1890/1 and then again in 1914/15. And in between these great achievements they won the FA Cup at the end of the 1905/6 season.

1892

Everton FC had always played on a corner of Stanley Park until the club grew a bit and it was decided to move to larger and better accommodation. The new venue was Anfield (now associated with another equally famous Merseyside club) but there appears to have been some sort of argument over the rent and so, in 1892, they upped sticks and moved a mile or two down the road to Goodison Park, which has been the Toffees' home ever since.

1907

For the second year running Everton reached the FA Cup final but were beaten 2–1 by Sheffield Wednesday.

1914/15

Everton finished the season as league champions again just before the competition was suspended for the duration of the war.

1927/8
Largely thanks to the legendary Dixie Dean, Everton had a glorious season and finished up as league champions, but . . .

1929/30
. . . what a fall from grace! In what has to be one of the most catastrophic turns of events in the history of the game, Everton ended the season and the bottom of the league and were relegated to the Second Division.

1930/1
Rising from the ashes Everton performed the impossible. Not only did they win promotion back to the First Division but they went from strength to strength and won the league again.

1940s and '50s
This was not a good time for the club. As football began to recover after the Second World War, Everton struggled to regain its former glory and in 1951 the team was relegated again to the Second Division. But this time there was to be no miraculous resurrection. It was not until 1954 that the team scrambled back into the First Division, although they did make it to the FA Cup finals in 1950 and 1953, only to be beaten first by Liverpool and then Bolton.

1960s and early '70s
This was a time when Everton players seemed to get a grip of themselves and make up for past mistakes. It was as if they had been asleep since the war and finally, if belatedly, woken up to the fact that, as footballers, they were expected to win the odd match. Now the trophies and honours came to Goodison thick and fast: league championship (1963), Charity Shield (1963), FA Cup (1966), league championship (1970), Charity Shield (1970).

Mid-1970s
Everything seemed to be going fine for the team at the start of the decade but then they ran out of steam. They put in some good performances but for most of the time the honours remained just out of reach.

1980s

One of the club's best decades! For much of the time the players did exactly what they were supposed to do: they went out onto the pitch and won. The only blot on their escutcheon during this period was a humiliating defeat by their arch-rivals Liverpool in November 1982 when they were thrashed in a 5–0 rout. However, they did win: the FA Cup (1984), Charity Shield (1984, 1985 and 1987), European Cup (1985) and league championship (1985 and 1987). They were also runners-up in the Milk Cup (1984) and FA Cup (1985 and 1986).

1990s

The slings and arrows of outrageous fortune gave the managers and players alike many sleepless nights during the whole decade. The first couple of seasons are best forgotten as, apart from a couple of fortuitous blips, the general trend, once again, was a downward one. The nadir was probably the 1994/5 season when, yet again, Everton only just avoided relegation. In the closing days of 1994 Joe Royle took over as manager and for a while it looked as though the fans' prayers had been answered: the team won the FA Cup in May 1995. But the rejoicing was brief as the 1997/8 season saw relegation again a distinct possibility. They only avoided relegation because they had a superior goal difference to Bolton Wanderers.

2000 onwards

Pretty much more of the same; some highs, many lows and relegation never a comfortable distance away. The best for the team during this period were the 2003/4 and 2004/5 seasons when they had some of the best results since 1988 but, generally speaking, a distinct lack of consistency characterised their overall performance. They did manage to end the 2009 season as runners-up in the FA Cup, but this was little consolation for players and fans alike. But there was worse to come. The 2010/11 season started disastrously and, not only did they fail to win a league match before October, but were knocked out of the League Cup by Brentford. By February 2011 things were not looking at all rosy and a 2–0 defeat by Bolton had the manager, David Moyes, complaining that his team had put in one of the worst performances he had ever seen. Relegation was rearing its ugly head again, but things improved and they finished the season in seventh position.

The club motto
Nil satis nisi optimum
which is Latin for:
Nothing satisfies but the best

Club managers
W.F. Barclay (Aug 1888–May1889)
Dick Molyneux (Aug 1889–May1901)
William Cuff (Aug 1901–May 1918)
W.J. Sawyer (Aug 1918–May 1919)
Thomas McIntosh (Aug 1919–May 1935)
From May 1935 to June 1939 the team had no manager but was run by a committee.
Theo Kelly (June 1939–Sep 1948)
Cliff Britton (Sep 1948–Feb 1956)
Ian Buchan (Feb 1956–Oct 1958)
Johnny Carey (Oct 1958–Apr 1961)
Harry Catterick (Apr 1961–Apr 1973)
Tom Eggleston (Apr 1973–May 1973)
Billy Bingham (Aug 1973–Jan 1977)
Steve Burtenshawe (10 Jan 1977–30 Jan 1977)
Gordon Lee (Feb 1977–May 1981)
Howard Kendall (Aug 1981–May 1987)
Colin Harvey (Aug 1987–Oct 1990)
Jimmy Gabriel (Nov 1990–Nov 1990)
Howard Kendall (Nov 1990–Dec 1993)
Jimmy Gabriel (Dec 1993–Jan 1994)
Mike Walker (Jan 1994–Nov 1994)
Joe Royle (Nov 1994–Mar 1997)
Dave Watson (Apr 1997–May 1997)
Howard Kendall (Aug 1997–May 1998)
Walter Smith (Aug 1998–Mar 2002)
David Moyes (Mar 2002–)

Some facts

Everton have never actually played in Everton. Its first home ground, Anfield, is in the Liverpool district of Anfield and Goodison Park is in Walton.

Dixie Dean's record of 60 league goals in one season (1927/28) has never been equalled.

LIVERPOOL HUMOUR: EXAMPLE FIFTEEN

Overheard on a bus
>Passenger: *Does this bus stop at the Pier Head?*
>Driver: *There'll be an 'ell of a splash if it doesn't.*

THE FOOTBALL LEAGUE

The Football League's first season began on 8 September 1888 with twelve clubs registered and considered the founding members. They were: Burnley, Accrington, Aston Villa, Blackburn Rovers, Bolton Wanderers, Everton, Derby County, Notts County, Stoke (Stoke City after 1928), Preston North End, Wolverhampton Wanderers and West Bromwich Albion.

LIVERPOOL FC

When the original team decided to up sticks and decamp to Goodison Park, the landowner and landlord of Anfield, John Houlding, was left with a vacant pitch on his hands, and vacant pitches do not bring in any rent. So he decided to form another club and, to cut a long story short, the new club eventually became the team we now know as Liverpool FC.

1892

As soon as the team formed it showed promise. The lads were gathered together in June for the first time and then went straight on to win the Lancashire League in their first season.

1893

They now joined the Football League, at Second Division level, and showed the same grit and talent that they had displayed in the Lancashire League. After only one season they finished in first place and were immediately promoted into the First Division.

1901 and 1906

League champions. But then there was a bit of an honours hiatus and an twenty years elapsed before the team brought any trophies back to Anfield.

1922 and 1923

League champions again, two seasons on the trot. But this was followed by yet another twenty-odd years without any honours.

1947

League champions again. But then things just seemed to go from bad to worse. There were no more trophies, no more honours and precious few wins. The downward slide had begun and nothing and nobody seemed capable of doing anything to stop it.

1954

For the first time in its fifty-odd year history the Reds found themselves relegated to the Second Division where they languished for the next seven years.

1959

This was the year when Liverpool reached what was probably its lowest point ever. On 15 January the non-league club Worcester City beat the Reds 2–1 and knocked them out of the FA Cup. The only consolation for Liverpool FC historians is that the defeat represented rock bottom and from now on the only way was up. Fortunately, this turned out to be the case.

1959–74

The fifteen years after the humiliating Worcester City débâcle were dominated by one man: Bill Shankly. He took the demoralised team and pulled it up by its bootstraps (certainly metaphorically and almost literally). He got rid of players who were past their sell-by date and introduced as much new blood as the team could afford. Whatever it was that was needed to transform a beaten team into European champions in a relatively short space of time, Shankly had it. And it brought home the silverware: league championship (1964 shared, 1966 and 1973), charity shield (1964 (shared), 1966 and 1974), FA Cup (1965 and 1974), UEFA Cup (1973). They were also runners-up in the Charity Shield (1965 and 1971), European Cup Winners' Cup (1966), league championship (1969 and 1974) and FA Cup (1971).

1974–83

Bill Shankly was a hard act to follow and, when he retired, the fans were understandably nervous about his successor. But they needn't have been – Bob Paisley turned out to be one of the most successful managers in the history of football. In the nine years he was in post there was only one season without a trophy and for most of the time it was difficult finding space on the mantelpiece: league champions (1976, 1977, 1979, 1980, 1982, 1983), UEFA Cup (1976), Charity Shield (1976, 1977 shared, 1979, 1980, 1982), European Cup (1977, 1978, 1981), League Cup (1981, 1982, 1983). The Reds were also runners-up in the league championship (1975, 1978), Charity Shield (1976), FA Cup (1977), League Cup (1978), European Super Cup (1978), Intercontinental Cup (1981).

1983–5

Although the 1983/4 season got off to a reasonable start, Joe Fagan's time in office was marred by the blackest day imaginable. On the pitch the team performed creditably, but this was a time when the mighty giant began to wobble. They suffered some surprise defeats by teams such as Coventry, who beat the Reds 4–0 in December 1983, and Sunderland who sent them back to the dressing room to lick their wounds after an unexpected 1–0 defeat. However, the event that marred the whole period was the Heysel Stadium tragedy. Liverpool supporters tore down the fence separating them from Juventus supporters and, in the ensuing confusion, a wall collapsed and 39 people were crushed to death. Liverpool supporters were branded as hooligans and all English clubs were banned from taking part in European football indefinitely. Joe Fagan had no choice but to resign.

However, there were some bright spots in all the gloom, and there were some memorable achievements. In 1984 Liverpool became the first club in the country to win three major titles in one season: the League Cup, the league championship and the European Cup. This was a stupendous feat but there was more to come as they also played well enough to be runners-up in the Charity Shield (1983 and 1984), Intercontinental Cup (1984), European Super Cup (1984), league championship (1985) and European Cup (1985).

1985–91

This was another period in the club's history that was marked by both triumph and tragedy. There was a fair amount of silverware brought home to adorn the boardroom at Anfield, even if the team had suffered some shock defeats on the way to acquiring it. But, in what seemed like an unbelievable reminder of the Heysel tragedy just a few years earlier, Liverpool fans were involved in the Hillsborough disaster.

Despite the tragedy, this period also saw a time of great rejoicing at Anfield as the Reds achieved what few teams had managed in the whole history of football – they won the FA Cup and were league champions in the same season. During Kenny Dalglish's time as manager the team honours were: league champions (1986, 1988, 1990), FA Cup (1986, 1989), Charity Shield (shared 1986, 1988, 1989 and then shared again in 1990).

1990s

Not the best time for Liverpool or Liverpool fans. The club did manage to win the FA Cup in 1992 and were league runners-up in 1991 as well as in the Charity Shield in 1992, but this was not a great showing for the team that had only recently brought so many honours home to Merseyside. By the end of the 1993/94 season the Reds had slumped to eighth in the league, the team's worst performance for almost thirty years. For the rest of the decade hopes of a dramatic improvement soon faded and it was not until the dawning of the new century that Liverpool FC began to show some of its old spark.

2000 onwards

The new millennium brought a temporary improvement in Liverpool's fortunes and the 2000/01 season was their best for years. The trophies once again were plentiful and the team's performance impressive enough to be the envy of just about every other team in the country: the League Cup (2001, 2003), the FA Cup (2001), UEFA Cup (2001), FA Charity Shield (2001) and UEFA Super Cup (2001). But, as ever, brilliant success was followed by a prolonged period of disappointment. In the 2003/04 season Liverpool went through their longest barren streak of not winning a single match. The manager, Gérard Houllier, was replaced by Rafael Benítez and yet again the spectres of success and failure continued to haunt the team. There were plenty of honours: the European Cup (2005), UEFA Super Cup (2005), FA Cup (2006), FA Community Shield (2006) and the team also finished as runners-up in the Carling Cup (2005), European Cup (2007) and the Premier League (2009). Unfortunately, by October 2010 the team had been playing so poorly that they were looking at relegation from the Premier League and had been knocked out of the League Cup. Then, to make matters worse, they were knocked out of the FA Cup in the third round in January 2011 by Manchester United. By the end of the season they could only manage sixth position.

The club motto
You'll Never Walk Alone

Club managers
W.E. Barclay, jointly with John McKenna (Feb 1892–Aug 1896)
Tom Watson (Aug 1896–May 1915)
David Ashworth (Dec 1919–Feb 1923)
Matt McQueen (Feb 1923–Feb 1928)
George Patterson (Mar 1928–Aug 1936)
George Kay (Aug 1936–Jan 1951)
Don Welsh (Mar 1951–May 1956)
Phil Taylor (May 1956–Nov 1959)
Bill Shankly (Dec 1959–July 1974)
Bob Paisley (Aug 1974–July 1983)
Joe Fagan (July 1983–May 1985)
Kenny Dalglish (May 1985–Feb 1991)
Ronnie Moran (Feb 1991–April 1991)
Graeme Souness (April 1991–Jan 1994)
Roy Evans (Jan 1994–Nov 1998)
Gérard Houllier (July 1998–May 2004)
Rafael Benítez (June 2004–June 2010)
Roy Hodgson (July 2010–Jan 2011)
Kenny Dalglish (Jan 2011–)

Some facts
In 1994 Liverpool forked out £400,000 for the Danish goalkeeper Michael Stensgaard but before he could play for the first team the Dane injured his shoulder when putting up an ironing board! The injury was so bad that he was classified as unfit to play and retired in 1996. He was twenty-one.

Billy Liddell, who played for Liverpool for twenty-two years, never played professionally for any other team. He retired in 1960.

THE 'CRÈME DE LA CRÈME'

Liverpool FC is up among the most successful sides in the history of football. The team has won 18 league titles, 7 FA Cups and 7 League Cups. The team has also won 5 European Cups and 3 UEFA Cups. The club is also recognised as having won the greatest number of international titles.

AN HISTORICAL INEXACTITUDE

Anyone who has ever spent any time in Liverpool knows that the old religious divisions of the city are somewhat reflected in the football. Traditionally Catholics supported Everton and Protestants supported Liverpool. But as both teams can trace their origins back to the same Methodist Church in St Domingo Road the dichotomy is not only pointless but historically inaccurate.

LIVERPOOL HUMOUR: EXAMPLE SIXTEEN

In the 1970s there were two old tramps who hung around the Soho Street and Islington area near the city centre. Nobody knew their names but locals nicknamed them 'Bacon and Eggs' because you never saw one without the other.

HORSE RACING

Long before football was even heard of, horse racing was a popular sport in and around Liverpool. The details are a little hazy, but we do know that races were run near Crosby and on Kirkdale Sands way back in Tudor times and that by the nineteenth century, Maghull had become a popular venue for riders and owners alike. There is some dispute as to when organised horse racing began in the area as racing of a casual sort was already popular in or near Aintree in the early nineteenth century. However, it is generally accepted now that the first official handicap chase was run at the Aintree course in 1839. And the person racegoers have to thank for the annual event is a certain William Lynn, the owner of the nearby Waterloo Hotel who rented the land from William Molyneux, the Earl of Sefton (hence the name of the pub which still adjoins the course, The Sefton).

When the news of the planned and professionally organised race reached the ears of the local aristocracy it caused a good deal of excitement. The well-to-do of Lancashire and the surrounding area seized on the event as an opportunity for a bit of fun. They could, and did, turn the whole enterprise into a holiday, combining the thrill of the race with ample supplies of victuals and lashings of liquid refreshment. Horse racing as serious entertainment had arrived on Merseyside and it has survived to the present day, despite two world wars, a depression and who knows how many recessions.

The favourite for the first ever Grand National was Conrad, ridden by Captain Becher. Unfortunately Conrad threw his rider twice and so the favourite came nowhere and the winner on the day was the not inappropriately named Lottery, ridden by Jem Mason. Captain Becher, however, did not disappear from history, even though he never rode in the race again. The obstacle where the horse threw his rider has ever since been known as Becher's Brook.

The course is known to be one of the most gruelling (some would say *the* most gruelling) steeplechase course anywhere in the world. It is basically triangular in shape, 4 miles 4 furlongs in length with sixteen fences for the horse to jump. Fourteen of

the fences have to be jumped twice with only two of the most formidable (the Chair and the Water Jump) challenging horse and rider just once. Becher's and the Chair are considered to be the most dangerous for horse and rider.

The sixteen obstacles or fences facing the riders at Aintree are of different heights and construction, but even the most innocuous of them must seem a formidable challenge to both horse and rider as they loom out of the distance:

Fence No. 1
4ft 6in high. In 1951 twelve horses, with their riders, fell at the first hurdle.

Fence No. 2
4ft 7in

Fence No. 3
5ft high with a 6ft ditch in front of it. This fence is known as the Westhead and is regarded by many jockeys as being the most feared. It is named after a Mr Westhead who at one time was a groundskeeper at Aintree.

Fence No. 4
4ft 10in

Fence No. 5
5ft high

Fence No. 6
This is the famous Becher's Brook. When the horse clears this 4ft 10in fence it is (unexpectedly) faced with a 6ft 9in drop on the other side. All but the most skilful (or brave) find this a little off-putting and for many this jump marks the end of the race.

Fence No. 7
At 4ft 6in this fence is the smallest on the whole course. Since 1984 it has been called the Foinavon fence in honour of a horse of the same name who won the race in spectacular fashion in 1967 at odds of 100/1.

Fence No. 8
Known as the Canal Turn. This one takes its name from the sudden 90-degree turn that horse and rider have to make once they have cleared the 5ft fence.

Fence No. 9
5ft high and known as Valentine's Brook after the horse which, as legend has it, cleared the jump on its hind legs in 1840.

Fence No. 10
This is just a plain 5ft high fence.

Fence No. 11
5ft high but with a 6ft ditch in front of it.

Fence No. 12
A 5ft 6in fence with a 6ft ditch but this time the ditch is on the landing side.

Fence No. 13
4ft 7in high.

Fence No. 14
4ft 6in high. This is the fence where horses have been known to fall, not because they were injured but because they were simply exhausted.

Fence No. 15
Known as the Chair, this is a 5ft 3in high fence with a 6ft ditch in front of it. This was where the 'distance judge' used to sit in the early days of the race. This official was dispensed with as long ago as the 1850s but the jump is still a reminder of where he sat to perform his duties.

Fence No. 16
The Water Jump. In the very early days of the race this was a ditch fronted by a low stone wall which has long since been replaced by a normal hedge jump. It is a mere 2ft high but followed immediately by a 10ft wide ditch.

CAPTAIN BECHER

Captain Martin William Becher (1797–1864) was a passionate horseman who served in the army during the Napoleonic Wars and might have taken part in the Battle of Waterloo but we cannot be certain. He was a friend of William Lynn and is thought to have given him the idea of holding the race which then developed into the Grand National. When his horse Conrad threw him at the hurdle which now bears his name, he is reported as having commented on how filthy the water tasted without the beneficial addition of a slug of whisky.

THE STEEPLECHASE

Q. Why is the Grand National known as a 'steeplechase?'

A. The answer is said to lie in County Cork, Ireland, where, in 1752, two gentlemen had a wager to see who could beat the other in a horse race. It was agreed that the start point would be the church steeple at Buttevant Church and the finish would be the steeple on St Leger's Church in Doneraile, just 4 miles away. The race was across rough terrain and involved the negotiation of fences, ditches and hedges and so the term 'steeplechase' came to define any race which included natural or man-made obstacles.

Some facts

The race was originally called the Grand Liverpool Steeplechase. In 1847 it became the Grand National Handicap Steeplechase and this is still officially the race's correct title.

In the history of the Grand National mares have won only thirteen times. The first was Charity in 1841 and the last was Nickel Coin in 1951.

The most successful horse in the history of the race is Red Rum with three wins (1973, 1974 and 1977).

During the First World War the race was transferred down south and run on land now covered over by Gatwick airport.

In 1968 the race was won by Red Alligator at 100/1. The favourite was Different Class, owned by the Hollywood star Gregory Peck.

For safety reasons no more than forty horses are allowed to enter the Grand National.

The event is so popular that it takes over 3,000 caterers to provide food and drink for the punters.

AND WHAT ABOUT THE OTHER SPORTS?

Mention the word 'Liverpool' and most people think of football; mention the word 'Aintree' and people all over the world immediately think of horse racing. So it tends to be easily forgotten that other sports have thrived on Merseyside for generations where world-class exponents of lesser-known sporting activities quietly indulge their passions, even though they seldom make it to the back pages of the national newspapers. Here are some:

Martial Arts

Virtually all the martial arts are catered for in and around Liverpool. What is generally not realised, however, is that some of the institutions where these noble and ancient arts are practised have a reputation which has spread far beyond the borders of the North-West. In fact, some are world class.

Take **jiu-jitsu**, for instance. In the 1950s James Blundell, a quiet man of diminutive stature, founded a club in Hayman's Green, West Derby, where he taught the jiu-jitsu skills he had acquired in the Far East. The Lowlands, as the club was called, developed and became the nucleus for what is now the British Jiu-Jitsu Association. Unfortunately, James is no longer with us but the club and the association continue to grow and flourish under the guidance of his son and grandson, Professor Kenneth Blundell and Sensei (teacher) Wayne Blundell.

Karate has long been popular in Liverpool and is still very much alive and kicking (pun definitely intended!). Their names might not be well-known among the general public, but there can few students of the art anywhere in the world who will not have heard of experts such as Andy Sherry and Terry O'Neill. And they are both Liverpool born and bred. Andy Sherry (born in 1943) began by studying jiu-jitsu in 1956 but then decided that the martial art he really wanted to study was karate. He studied seriously and eventually became the first person in the country to be awarded a black belt in the shotokan style. In the 1960s and '70s he won a string of national and international titles and was many times a member of the winning UK or England team. Now retired from competition, Andy Sherry still coaches at international level and is Chairman of the Karate Union of Great Britain. He was recently awarded the rank of 8th Dan and is thus the highest graded karateka in Britain.

A pupil of Andy Sherry, Terry O'Neill (born in 1948) is another martial arts expert who learned his trade in his native Liverpool before going on to achieve great things. He was KUGB National Champion (1972, 1973, 1974, 1975, 1977 and 1978) and three times KUGB Grand Champion. He also captained the UK team that, amazingly, beat the Japanese squad and then went on to win the World Championships in 1975. But Terry O'Neill has added a second dimension to his karate career: in films and on TV. He has taken on fighting roles and appeared alongside stars such as Sean Connery, Michael Caine and Arnold Schwarzenegger. Films in which he has either displayed his formidable talents or acted as consultant include: *The League of Extraordinary Gentlemen* (2003), *Gangs of New York* (2002), *The Man Who Knew Too Little* (1997) and *Conan the Destroyer* (1984).

Cycling

Born in 1944 another Scouser who has become a bit of a legend in his sport of choice is **Douglas James Dailey**. He was awarded a well-deserved MBE in 2008 for his contribution to a sport which is far more popular on and around Merseyside than most people realise. He grew up in the Orrell Park area of the city, the son of a staunchly left-wing local politician and when he left school (Hillfoot Hey High) in the late 1950s his first job was with BICC in Prescot. However, he hated every minute of it and fairly soon decided that enough was enough. His love of cycling drew him in the direction of making the sport his career and this is exactly what he did; BICC's loss was definitely British cycling's gain. As a competitor he went on to be the British National Road Race Champion in 1972 and 1976 and then, in 1969 and 1984, he won the Merseyside Golden Cycle Award. When he retired from competition he moved over to the administration side of things where his contribution has been no less and he is now involved with organising the cycling events for the 2012 London Olympics. Doug Dailey's name has also been included in the British Cycling Hall of Fame.

Chris Boardman is another well-known name among the racing fraternity. He was born in Hoylake on the Wirral in 1968 and developed a passion for sport in general and cycling in particular at an early age. And his devotion and determination have paid off: he has amassed a string of awards and honours over the years which make the successes of all but the greatest athletes pale into insignificance. He has achieved much in the Olympics, the Tour de France and competitions organised closer to home. In 1988, 1989 and 1990 he won the United Kingdom National Hill Climb Championships and came second in 1987. In 1991 he won both the UK National Hill Climb Championships and the National Amateur Track Pursuit Championship. The latter competition he also won again in 1992.

In 2000, just before his retirement, Boardman also went on to perform magnificently in the Hour Record (a competition to see who can cover the greatest distance in a timed hour) when he achieved what many thought was impossible. He covered a distance of 34.9 miles, beating the 30.6 miles record set by the legendary Belgian rider Eddie Merckx.

In 1992 Chris was awarded the MBE for his services to cycling and in 1997 an Honorary Doctorate from Brighton University for services to Sports Science. In 2009 his name was included in the British Cycling Hall of Fame.

Boxing

Boxing has been a popular sport in Liverpool since the nineteenth century (and possibly even earlier) and the city has produced some outstanding fighters, including:

Nelson (aka 'Nel') Tarleton (1906–56) was a Liverpool lad who won the featherweight championship three times and did not retire from the ring until he was forty-two years old. He won the Lonsdale belt twice, which put him in the class of only seven boxers who won the belt more than once. During his long career he had 144 fights, won 116 and drew 8. But the most amazing fact about this tall, gangly fighter is that he only had one lung!

John Conteh (b. 1951) hails from Kirkby. He was introduced to boxing at a very early age when his father, who was not a boxer himself, was able to instruct him in the basics. As an amateur John went on to win three gold medals at the Commonwealth games and then ABA middleweight titles in 1970 and WBC light heavyweight in 1971. When he turned professional he was so good that there was talk of a match between him and Muhammad Ali, but this never materialised. Nevertheless, John Conteh did become holder of the World Boxing Council's World Crown in 1973 and during his career chalked up 34 wins with 1 draw and just 4 losses . . . a pretty impressive record.

Paul Smith (b. 1982) took up boxing as a boy aged just nine and learned his trade at the Rotunda Boxing Club in the Kirkdale area of the city. He fights at super middleweight level and won the British Championship title for his weight in 2009 and then successfully defended it in 2010. Paul Smith fights mainly in Liverpool and Manchester but has also taken on opponents in places as far afield as USA, Denmark and Uzbekistan. In 2002 he won the silver medal (boxing as a light middleweight) at the Commonwealth Games and to date he has had a total of 31 professional fights with 29 wins (15 of them by knock-out), he has lost 2 and drawn none.

Alan Rudkin. In September 2010 Liverpool and the whole country suddenly lost a boxer who, in the opinion of many, was one of the best athletes ever to step into a boxing ring. Alan Rudkin displayed a natural talent for boxing and was widely acknowledged in the sporting world as the best British boxer who never won a world title. He was born in North Wales in 1941 (his mother had been evacuated from Liverpool because of the bombing) but was brought up in the Dingle area. As a child he contracted polio and his family was warned that the chances of his ever walking again were pretty slim. However, not only did he learn to walk again but went on to become a very talented amateur and successful professional boxer. Between 1965 and 1970 he won the British, Commonwealth and European bantamweight championships and in a ten-year professional career (1962–72) won 42 out of a total of 50 fights. He was awarded the MBE for his achievements in 1980. In 2008, when the city of Liverpool was celebrating 800 years of history, the *Liverpool Echo* included Alan Rudkin in its list of the 800 greatest Liverpudlians.

9

LIVERPOOL'S LITERATI

All societies tell stories. From the dawn of time men (and women) have allowed their imaginations to conjure up tales and myths to entertain, inform, amuse and sometimes to control others. At first the stories were passed on orally but then, as technology advanced, writing was developed which allowed the imaginings of man to be set down, read by others and passed on to successive generations. And Liverpool was no exception; as a more educated and leisured class began to evolve it produced writers who recorded the tragedies, triumphs, hopes and aspirations of their native city. And when the twentieth century brought the invention of television, many Liverpool scribes found a new and immediate outlet for their gritty social commentary and stark realism.

THE POETS

Felicia Hemans

Few people will know the name Felicia Hemans. And even fewer will have heard of the poem entitled 'Casabianca'. But just about everybody in the English speaking world knows the line, 'The boy stood on the burning deck . . .'. So it might come as a bit of a surprise to know that Felicia Hemans, 'Casabianca' and the famous line of poetry are all connected – indeed the phrase is the poem's first line. She was a prolific poet, befriended and admired by some of the great Romantic poets of the age including Byron, Shelley and Wordsworth, but for some reason she has faded from the pages of literary history.

Felicia Hemans was born Felicia Dorothea Browne in Duke Street, Liverpool, then an area of refined affluence, in 1793, and wrote 'Casabianca' in her thirties, recalling the fate of Captain Casabianca, who was killed at the Battle of the Nile (1799). The 'boy' in question was the captain's twelve-year-old son who refused to leave his dying father even though the ship was ablaze and he knew he faced certain death. Unaccountably, there is no memorial to the poet anywhere in her native Liverpool, but she is remembered and revered in America on the strength of another of her poems, 'The Landing of the Pilgrim Fathers', which is a standard text in many US schools and is traditionally recited at Thanksgiving ceremonies. She died in 1835.

Roger McGough CBE

Roger Joseph McGough CBE was born in 1937 in Litherland. He was educated locally and then went on to study French at Hull University. On graduating he taught for a while but soon decided that his heart was not in the classroom and preferred to be writing and reciting poetry. Liverpool, and the country as a whole, has been the richer for his decision.

In the 1960s he collaborated with other Scouse luminaries of the generation such as Adrian Henri and Brian Patten and went on to be one of the most prolific (and original) poets the country has ever produced. His work has been criticised for not being high-brow enough, but it is witty, engaging, amusingly sarcastic at times and always entertaining. His manipulation of the English language is unequalled as is his ability to make the reader stop and reconsider words he or she has used unthinkingly all his or her life.

Awards, quite rightly, have been showered upon him and include the Signal Poetry Award (1984 and 1999), the Royal Television Society Award (1993), an OBE (1997), a CBE (2008) and the Cholmondeley Award (1998). He has also been awarded a string of honorary academic awards from various universities. In 2001 he was granted the Freedom of the City of Liverpool. Roger McGough presents the BBC radio programme *Poetry Please*. In December 2011 Roger McGough was elected President of the Poetry Society.

LIVERPOOL HUMOUR: EXAMPLE SEVENTEEN

To describe somebody as being unequal to a given task a Scouser might say:

Yer about as much use as an inflatable dartboard

or

Yer about as much use as a water-proof tea bag

THE NOVELISTS

Nicholas Monsarrat

Nicholas Monsarrat is probably best known for his novel *The Cruel Sea* (1951) which was made into an extremely successful film starring such stalwarts of the British film industry as Jack Hawkins, Donald Sinden and Stanley Baker. Nicholas John Turney Monsarrat was born in Rodney Street in 1910 to well-to-do parents (his father was a prominent surgeon). After he graduated in Law at Cambridge it was naturally assumed that young Nicholas would enter the legal profession but it was not to be. He was not cut out to be a barrister; he found the work uninteresting and resolved that he would become a writer. He began by writing for newspapers and trying his hand at novels. When war broke out in 1939 he found himself in something of a moral quandary as he wanted to 'do his bit', but at the same time was a confirmed pacifist. He found a solution to his self-imposed dilemma by deciding to help win the war and then worry about his moral convictions. To this end he joined the Royal Naval Reserves and served in a corvette helping protect the Atlantic convoys. His experiences gave him much material for a series of novels about life on the ocean waves, including *The Cruel Sea*. Ostensibly this is a tale of derring-do involving the British Navy's struggle against the threat of German U-boats. But, at a deeper level, it deals with man's struggle against the forces of nature and how ordinary, apparently insignificant people can display unsuspected bravery, fortitude and resilience in the face of extreme danger.

When the war was over Nicholas Monsarrat entered the Diplomatic Service. This provided yet another source for his literary material and he went on to write *The Ship that Died of Shame* (1959), *The Tribe That Lost Its Head* (1956) and *Richer Than All His Tribe* (1968). Another novel, *The Story of Esther Costello* (1952) caused a certain amount of controversy and was not well received in certain quarters. It was interpreted as an unflattering account of the Helen Keller story and seen as an attack on American fund-raising tactics. The novel was made into a film starring Joan Crawford but the film, along with the novel, raised hackles and almost led to legal action.

When Nicholas Monsarrat died in 1979 his wish was to be buried at sea and the Royal Navy was honoured to comply with his request.

Brian Jacques

Brian Jacques enjoyed the kind of success story most writers can only dream about. He was born in Kirkdale in 1939, the son of a lorry driver and had nothing more than a rudimentary education and left school at the age of fifteen. But despite his humble academic beginnings his passion for literature was evident at a very early age. As a boy he read voraciously, and his reading matter was not rubbish; he revelled in the classics. He loved popular stories such as the Sherlock Holmes adventures, *Tarzan* and *Treasure Island* but also derived a great deal of pleasure from reading the heavier stuff such as Homer's *The Iliad* and *The Odyssey*. When he first tried his hand at writing, at the age of ten, his début story had a mixed reception. He had been told to write a story by his teacher who was then astounded at the quality of the young prodigy's work. It was so good that the teacher refused to believe Brian had not copied the story and demanded to know where he had got it from. Brian stuck to his guns and insisted that it was all his own work. The teacher stuck to *his* guns, insisting that it was an example of infant plagiarism and caned him for being a liar. Such institutionalised sadism was permitted in those days.

When he left school, Jacques did what many Liverpool lads did: he joined the Merchant Navy and travelled the world. When he gave up sailing the seven seas he had various jobs: lorry driver, docker, boxer and postman. And it was while working as a lorry driver that he wrote what was to be his breakthrough into the world of children's literature. His Redwall series was an immediate success, selling in its millions and being translated into dozens of languages. After this came collections of short stories such as *Seven Strange and Ghostly Tales* and *The Ribbajack & Other Curious Yarns*. Another series of books came under the heading of Castaways of the Flying Dutchman and he also found time to write the play *Brown Bitter, Wet Nellies and Scouse*, which was performed at the Everyman Theatre in 1981.

Liverpool University recognised Brian Jacques's achievements when they awarded him an Honorary Doctorate of Letters in 2005. In the same year he was also given an Honorary Fellowship from LJMU. He died in 2011.

Beryl Bainbridge

Dame Beryl Margaret Bainbridge was born in Liverpool in 1932 and raised in Formby, where her father was a reasonably successful businessman until he fell upon hard times and was declared bankrupt. At school she was, by all accounts, a bright but somewhat unruly child. She passed the scholarship and went to Merchant Taylors' grammar school but was invited to leave when she was found to be in possession of a piece of paper on which a rude limerick was written. We might suspect, however, that this episode was more a case of the last straw breaking the camel's back as Beryl had never been what we might call a docile pupil. She had acquired the nickname 'Basher Bainbridge' because of her tendency to get into fights; she herself claimed that she would take on the whole form if she had to.

After school Beryl set her sights on becoming an actress and made her stage début at the Liverpool Playhouse in 1948. She was still making a living as an actress when, in 1961, she appeared in television's *Coronation Street* as a 'ban the bomb' protester.

Her first published novel, *A Weekend with Claude*, appeared in 1967, although the first novel she wrote was *Harriet Said . . .* which was not published until 1972. At this point in her life she was not a happy woman; relationships had turned sour and she retreated more and more into what might be described as a cross between a bohemian and eccentric lifestyle. Her house in Camden (London) had a stuffed buffalo in the hall and a life-size model of Neville Chamberlain sitting by the window in her bedroom. But the odd surroundings appear to have encouraged her creativity as it was at this time that she produced what some consider her best writing, *The Dressmaker* (1973), *The Bottle Factory Outing* (1974) and *Injury Time* (1977). Beryl died in 2010.

Frederick Nolan

Frederick Nolan was born in Liverpool in 1931 and has spent just about all of his working life on both sides of publishing: he has written prolifically and was employed by some of the world's major publishing houses in advisory and executive roles. He was determined from an early age that he wanted to be a writer, but it took him the best part of thirty years to actually get round to doing anything about it. In the meantime he had to put bread on the table and to this end he worked as a typewriter salesman, a shipping clerk and even as one of those people who decorate chocolates on a conveyor belt before they get put into little boxes prior to leaving the factory.

As a reader his choice of genre was the Western and his passion for reading (and later for writing) about the American wild west was apparently limitless. In fact, so thorough was his research into the life led by the cowboys that he became a recognised authority on the subject, his particular interest being the life, times and death of William Bonney, aka Billy the Kid.

Since the 1960s Frederick Nolan has demonstrated a remarkable ability to produce exactly the kind of book that the public wants to read and several have enjoyed spectacular success. In 1973 he resigned his executive position in publishing to become a full-time author and his novel *The Oshawa Project* (published in the USA as *The Algonquin Project*) was made into the film *Brass Target* staring Sophia Loren, John Cassavetes, Robert Vaughan and other well-known stars of stage and screen.

He has used several *noms-de-plume* for the various genres in which he works including Christine Maguire and Daniel Rockfern. For his Western series about a character called Sudden (originally created by Oliver Strange) he chose the pseudonym Frederick H. Christian.

LIVERPOOL HUMOUR: EXAMPLE EIGHTEEN

Jimmy's wife could sing a jewett (duet) all on 'er own
James's wife is a rather large lady

THE SCRIPTWRITERS

Phil Redmond

Nobody who has ever switched on a television set could deny the contribution Liverpool writers have made to the medium. And Phil Redmond in particular is up among those whose input has been greatest. He was born in Liverpool in 1949 and brought up on a housing estate in Huyton where life was not known for its ease and luxury. He passed the 11+ but, instead of going on to a grammar school, found himself in an unrealistically oversized comprehensive school (St Kevin's in Kirkby) where discipline was probably not as rigorous as it could have been. By his own admission his academic achievements were modest, but at least his experiences at the school provided a wealth of material on which he was able to draw later for scripts and storylines in programmes such as *Grange Hill* and *Hollyoaks. Grange Hill* was a long-running and popular series about school life, while *Hollyoaks* deals with the lives of youngsters and Redmond has never avoided dramatic and divisive storylines in either series. Phil Redmond argued that he wanted to get away from Enid Blyton and Billy Bunter and present his viewers with a more realistic exposé of teenage life. Not everybody thinks this makes for suitable viewing, but then Redmond has never been one to back down from controversy.

Outside the classroom, of course, his main drama series was *Brookside*. This was set in a real housing development in West Derby, Liverpool, and was another series in which the harsher problems of daily life were dealt with. Viewers watched as characters came to terms with unemployment, abortion, murder, drugs and homosexuality as well as 'normal' everyday matters such a family feuds, illicit affairs and relationship breakdowns. In many ways, it was *Grange Hill* for grow-ups: hard-hitting, tragic, shocking and simultaneously disturbing but addictive viewing.

Phil Redmond's achievements and contribution to both Liverpool and the media have been recognised. He was awarded the CBE in 2004 for his contribution to drama and he was elected Honorary Professor of Media Studies at LJMU in 1989.

Lynda La Plante

Lynda La Plante was born Lynda Titchmarsh just outside Liverpool (where her father was a salesman) in 1943. She married another writer, Richard La Plante, which explains her rather exotic surname, but the marriage broke up in the 1990s. Her first incarnation was as an actress where she studied at such august institutions as the Royal Academy of Dramatic Arts and then worked with the National Theatre and the Royal Shakespeare Company. Then she made the transition to television and those old enough to remember such ground-breaking police dramas of the 1960s and '70s such as *Z-Cars*, *The Professionals* and *Bergerac* just might remember her appearance under her then stage-name Lynda Marchal. She also appeared for a while as one of the ghosts in the popular, long-running children's series *Rentaghost* (1976–84).

But it was when she decided to turn to writing that her true talent shone through. She wrote her first TV script in the 1970s, *The Kids from 47A*, a children's programme. Then came the scripts for grown-ups: *Widows* (1983) and *Prime Suspect* (1991) which introduced Detective Chief Inspector Jane Tennison, played by Dame Helen Mirren, setting the seal on her reputation as one of TV's premier league writers. But Lynda La Plante was not the kind of girl to be satisfied with past successes and the 1990s saw a torrent of successful scripts flow from her metaphorical quill: *The Governor* (1995/6), *Trial and Retribution* (1997 onwards), *Bella Mafia* (1997) and *Killer Net* (1998).

As a writer she has also produced many fine novels such as *The Legacy*, *The Talisman* and *Silent Scream*, to name but a few. Lynda La Plante was appointed CBE in 2008.

Carla Lane

Born Romana Barrack in Liverpool in 1937, Carla Lane is another outstanding writer who made her name in television, although these days she is equally renowned for the work she does for unwanted or injured animals at her Sussex sanctuary. The thematic thread running through Carla Lane's work tends not to be the 'socialist realism' obsession with the harsher aspects of urban living. Or, at least, such themes are not dealt with in such a relentlessly dismal manner. She prefers to examine the complexities of relationships by focussing on the humour which can be extracted from human behaviour even when the protagonists are experiencing the stresses of everyday life. The interpersonal relationships between members of the same family are her particular forte. Her first major success in the world of television was *The Liver Birds* which centred around two Liverpool girls sharing a flat in the 1970s. The dramatic element and humour of the series develop from the girls' concern with and attitudes to boys, fashion, hairstyles, etc.

Another extremely popular series was *Butterflies* (1978–83), starring Wendy Craig. Here again, Carla Lane is keen to show the world as seen through the eyes of a normal woman. She is not the twisted soul of the type so beloved of many other writers, but just a normal housewife and mum (although one who never mastered the art of cooking!) who, quite simply, gets bored with hum-drum suburban life and is painfully aware that life is passing her by. The 'butterflies' of the titles refer to her husband's consuming hobby and the fact that he seems more interested in lepidoptera than he is in his wife. They also symbolise how the wife, Ria, feels that she, too, is trapped and not allowed to 'spread her wings' in the way she would like to.

However, it was *Bread* (1986–91) which many consider to be Carla Lane's writing at its best. Again it was a series centred around the various members of one Liverpool family. This time the setting is Liverpool 8 (Toxteth) where an ordinary, working-class family tries to cope with the difficulties of surviving in the 1980s under Margaret Thatcher's premiership. As with her earlier scripts, the author is at pains here to see the humour lying behind the harsh realities of life, relationships and the general struggle involved in getting up in the morning and making sure you can survive till it's time to go to bed again.

Since the late 1980s Cara Lane has concentrated more on the other passion in her life: animal rights.

LIKE PEAS IN A POD

Two contemporary Liverpudlian writers who are often mistaken for each other because of their uncannily similar physical appearance (grey hair, grey beard) are Alan Bleasdale and Willy Russell. They were born within a year of each other, both had humble backgrounds and both proved that if you have talent, the lack of a silver spoon in your mouth at the time of your birth is no handicap.

Alan Bleasdale was born in Liverpool in 1946 and went to school in Huyton and then moved on to grammar school in Widnes. When the time came for him to choose a career he went on to Padgate College of Education in Warrington where he qualified as a teacher. In the early 1970s he returned to Huyton to embark on his career in the classroom, but he was not there long before he decided that he needed a change of scenery and a greater change of scenery would be difficult to imagine. He took himself and his family off to the other side of the world and spent the next three years teaching in a school on the Gilbert and Ellice Islands (Now renamed Kiribati) in the South Pacific. He stayed there for three years and then came home to Liverpool where he took up a teaching post in Halewood.

However, he was not satisfied. He had the writer's itch and set pen to paper and within a short space of time was creating some of the most memorable characters in contemporary literature. His first venture into the world of fiction was with a character called Scully, a Liverpool lad who became the eponymous hero of the play *Scully's New Year's Eve* (1978). However, it was with *The Boys from the Blackstuff* (1982) that Bleasdale really made his mark. The 'black stuff' was the tarmac laid by the gang of workers who form the central nucleus of the play. But it was probably the character Yosser Hughes (magnificently portrayed by Bernard Hill in the TV version) and his constantly repeated invocation 'gizza job' which made the play so memorable. It not only summed up Yosser's plight as a man on the dole with a family to feed, but also captured the ethos of the decade. This was Thatcher's Britain and thousands of men on Merseyside found themselves out of work through no fault of their own. Yosser's plea was their plea.

Alan Bleasdale's other acclaimed dramas include *The Monocled Mutineer* (1986), *GBH* (1991), *Jake's Progress* (1995) and his most recent *The Sinking of the Laconia* (2011).

Willy Russell was born in Whiston in 1947. He too was from a relatively modest background but he benefitted from having parents who valued education and encouraged him to read from an early age. Unfortunately, the benefits of this tactic, in terms of a formal education, were not immediately obvious. He left school with just one 'O' level although it was, significantly, in English.

His first job was as a trainee ladies' hairdresser, a calling for which he seems to have been not entirely unsuited as he did eventually open his own salon. But the prospect of shampooing and setting his way through life did not appeal; he began writing songs in his spare time, most of which enjoyed a favourable reception in the folk clubs around Liverpool. Then, at the age of twenty, he decided he wanted another crack at getting an education and enrolled as a student at Liverpool Hope University. This was followed by a stint as a teacher in Toxteth.

However, like his contemporary Alan Bleasdale, he was convinced that there was a playwright inside him trying to get out. His first successful play *John, Paul, George, Ringo . . . and Bert* was staged in London's West End in 1974. It was almost certainly his experiences as a hairdresser that gave him the idea for *Educating Rita* (1980) which started life as a stage play and then was made into a film starring Sir Michael Caine and Julie Walters. It enjoyed phenomenal success as a portrayal of a young married woman (a hairdresser) who is convinced she could benefit from an Open University course just as well as any product of the educational system which catered mainly for those from a middle class background.

In a similar vein another of Willy Russell's astounding successes was *Shirley Valentine* (1986, then a film in 1989). This time the central character does not yearn for a better education but release from the soul-destroying routine of marriage. An unexpected opportunity allows her to go off on holiday to Greece where she has a *eureka* moment: the unfulfilled suburban housewife realises that there is more to life than frying egg and chips for her dull, unexciting husband. Suddenly she falls victim to dramatically contrasting possibilities: a life of romance and leisure on a sun-soaked Greek island or the day-in, day-out monotony of the pots and pans of life in Liverpool. The experience leaves her a changed woman.

LIVERPOOL HUMOUR: EXAMPLE NINETEEN

Mickey's stayin' at the Waldorf Astoria for a bit
Michael is at present a guest of Her Majesty in Walton Prison

BIBLIOGRAPHY

Aughton, Peter, *Liverpool, A People's History*, Carnegie Publishing Ltd, 2003

Belcham, John (ed.) *Liverpool 800: Character, Culture & History*, Liverpool University Press, 2006

Chandler, George, *Liverpool*, B.T. Batsford Books, 1957

Channon, Howard, *Portrait of Liverpool*, Robert Hale Ltd, 1970

Charters, David, *Liverpool, A World in One City*, The Bluecoat Press, 2003

Fletcher, Mike, *The Making of Liverpool*, Wharncliffe Books, 2004

Harding, Stephen, *Viking Mersey: Scandinavian Wirral, West Lancashire and Chester*, Countyvise Ltd, 2002

Lane, Linacre, and Spiegl, Fritz (ed.), *Lern Yerself Scouse*, Scouse Press, 1979

Minard, Brian, and Spiegl, Fritz (ed.), *Lern Yerself Scouse*, Scouse Press, 1972

Morgan, Kenneth O., *Oxford Illustrated History of Britain*, Oxford University Press, 1989

Muir, Ramsay, *A History of Liverpool*, Liverpool University Press, 1907

Rothwell, Catherine, *Liverpool in Old Photographs*, Sutton Publishing Limited, 1996

Ross, David, *England: History of a Nation,* Geddes and Grosset, 2005

Sharples, Joseph, *Liverpool*, Yale University Press, 2004

Walton-on-the-Hill History Group, *The Township of Walton*, self-published

Whynne-Hammond, Charles, *English Place-names Explained*, Countryside Books, 2005

Websites
www.wikipedia.org
www.bbc.co.uk/history
www.localhistories.org
Mike Royden's Local History pages
E. Chambré Hardman Archive

ACKNOWLEDGEMENTS

I would like to thank the friendly staff of the Liverpool Records Office who came to my help on a couple of occasions and provided me with interesting snippets of information which I have included in this book.

I also must say a big thank you to my wife, Jean, and daughter Kirstine Borrello who between them produced most of the drawings contained within these pages. My own attempts were pathetic and so I was completely reliant on their artistic talents to come to my rescue.

My sister Margaret Dermott, who now lives near Southport, was also a wonderful source of inspiration and information. She was excited by the project from the very beginning and provided many useful leads and suggestions which I was able to make use of. I was also able to rely on her to correct me when my own knowledge of our native city proved wanting, so . . . *many thanks, Sis.*

Last but not least I have to thank Michelle Tilling of The History Press both for offering me the project and for putting up with my numerous telephone calls when I needed advice.

Other titles published by The History Press

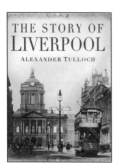

The Story of Liverpool
Alexander Tulloch
978-07509-4508-0
From its very beginnings Liverpool has always been associated with the ups and downs of the rest of the country. The history, the plots and the characters are brought to life in this fully illustrated, comprehensive and revealing account of the city's development.

800 Years of Haunted Liverpool
John Reppion
978-07524-4700-1
This creepy collection of true-life tales takes the reader on a tour through the streets, cemeteries, alehouses, attics and docks of Liverpool. Copiously illustrated with photographs, maps and drawings, this book will delight anyone with an interest in the supernatural history of the area. It is the first complete guide to the paranormal history of the region.

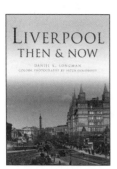

Liverpool Then & Now
Daniel K. Longman
978-07524-5740-6
The popular tourist city of Liverpool has a rich heritage, which is uniquely reflected in this fascinating new compilation. Contrasting a selection of archive images alongside full-colour modern photographs, this book delves into the changing faces and buildings of Liverpool.

Visit our website and discover thousands of other History Press books.

www.thehistorypress.co.uk